MACMILLAN MASTER GUIDES

GENERAL EDITOR: JAMES GIBSON

Published

JANE AUSTEN	*Emma* Norman Page
	Sense and Sensibility Judy Simons
	Pride and Prejudice Raymond Wilson
	Mansfield Park Richard Wirdnam
SAMUEL BECKETT	*Waiting for Godot* Jennifer Birkett
WILLIAM BLAKE	*Songs of Innocence* and *Songs of Experience* Alan Tomlinson
ROBERT BOLT	*A Man for all Seasons* Leonard Smith
EMILY BRONTË	*Wuthering Heights* Hilda D. Spear
GEOFFREY CHAUCER	*The Miller's Tale* Michael Alexander
	The Pardoner's Tale Geoffrey Lester
	The Knight's Tale Anne Samson
	The Prologue to the Canterbury Tales Nigel Thomas and Richard Swan
CHARLES DICKENS	*Bleak House* Dennis Butts
	Great Expectations Dennis Butts
	Hard Times Norman Page
GEORGE ELIOT	*Middlemarch* Graham Handley
	Silas Marner Graham Handley
	The Mill on the Floss Helen Wheeler
HENRY FIELDING	*Joseph Andrews* Trevor Johnson
E. M. FORSTER	*Howards End* Ian Milligan
	A Passage to India Hilda D. Spear
WILLIAM GOLDING	*The Spire* Rosemary Sumner
	Lord of the Flies Raymond Wilson
OLIVER GOLDSMITH	*She Stoops to Conquer* Paul Ranger
THOMAS HARDY	*The Mayor of Casterbridge* Ray Evans
	Tess of the d'Urbervilles James Gibson
	Far from the Madding Crowd Colin Temblett-Wood
JOHN KEATS	*Selected Poems* John Garrett
PHILIP LARKIN	*The Whitsun Weddings* and *The Less Deceived* Andrew Swarbrick
D. H. LAWRENCE	*Sons and Lovers* R. P. Draper
HARPER LEE	*To Kill a Mockingbird* Jean Armstrong
GERARD MANLEY HOPKINS	*Selected Poems* R.J.C. Watt
CHRISTOPHER MARLOWE	*Doctor Faustus* David A. Male
THE METAPHYSICAL POETS	Joan van Emden

MACMILLAN MASTER GUIDES

THOMAS MIDDLETON and WILLIAM ROWLEY	*The Changeling* Tony Bromham
ARTHUR MILLER	*The Crucible* Leonard Smith *Death of a Salesman* Peter Spalding
GEORGE ORWELL	*Animal Farm* Jean Armstrong
WILLIAM SHAKESPEARE	*Richard II* Charles Barber *Hamlet* Jean Brooks *King Lear* Francis Casey *Henry V* Peter Davison *The Winter's Tale* Diana Devlin *Julius Caesar* David Elloway *Macbeth* David Elloway *Measure for Measure* Mark Lilly *Henry IV Part I* Helen Morris *Romeo and Juliet* Helen Morris *The Tempest* Kenneth Pickering *A Midsummer Night's Dream* Kenneth Pickering *Coriolanus* Gordon Williams *Antony and Cleopatra* Martin Wine
GEORGE BERNARD SHAW	*St Joan* Leonée Ormond
RICHARD SHERIDAN	*The School for Scandal* Paul Ranger *The Rivals* Jeremy Rowe
ALFRED TENNYSON	*In Memoriam* Richard Gill
JOHN WEBSTER	*The White Devil* and *The Duchess of Malfi* David A. Male
VIRGINIA WOOLF	*To the Lighthouse* John Mepham *Mrs Dalloway* Julian Pattison

Forthcoming

CHARLOTTE BRONTË	*Jane Eyre* Robert Miles
JOHN BUNYAN	*The Pilgrim's Progress* Beatrice Batson
JOSEPH CONRAD	*The Secret Agent* Andrew Mayne
T. S. ELIOT	*Murder in the Cathedral* Paul Lapworth *Selected Poems* Andrew Swarbrick
BEN JONSON	*Volpone* Michael Stout
RUDYARD KIPLING	*Kim* Leonée Ormond
JOHN MILTON	*Comus* Tom Healy
WILLIAM SHAKESPEARE	*Othello* Tony Bromham *As You Like It* Kiernan Ryan
ANTHONY TROLLOPE	*Barchester Towers* Ken Newton
W. B. YEATS	*Selected Poems* Stan Smith

MACMILLAN MASTER GUIDES
THE KNIGHT'S TALE
BY GEOFFREY CHAUCER

ANNE SAMSON

MACMILLAN
EDUCATION

© Anne Samson 1987

All rights reserved. No reproduction, copy or transmission
of this publication may be made without written permission.

No paragraph of this publication may be reproduced, copied
or transmitted save with written permission or in accordance
with the provisions of the Copyright Act 1956 (as
amended), or under the terms of any licence permitting
limited copying issued by the Copyright Licensing Agency,
7 Ridgmount Street, London WC1E 7AE.

Any person who does any unauthorised act in relation to
this publication may be liable to criminal prosecution and
civil claims for damages.

First edition 1987

Published by
MACMILLAN EDUCATION LTD
Houndmills, Basingstoke, Hampshire RG21 2XS
and London
Companies and representatives
throughout the world

Typeset in Great Britain by
TEC SET, Wallington, Surrey

Printed in Hong Kong

British Library Cataloguing in Publication Data
Samson, Anne
The knight's tale by Geoffrey Chaucer —
(Macmillan master guides)
1. Chaucer, Geoffrey. Knight's tale
I. Title   II. Chaucer, Geoffrey. Knight's tale
821′.1   PR1868.K63
ISBN 0–333–42233–3 Pbk
ISBN 0–333–42234–1 Pbk export

CONTENTS

GENERAL EDITOR'S PREFACE

The aim of the Macmillan Master Guides is to help you to appreciate the book you are studying by providing information about it and by suggesting way of reading and thinking about it which will lead to a fuller understanding. The section on the writer's life and background has been designed to illustrate those aspects of the writer's life which have influenced the work, and to place it in its personal and literary context. The summaries and critical commentary are of special importance in that each brief summary of the action is followed by an examination of the significant critical points. The space which might have been given to repetitive explanatory notes has been devoted to a detailed analysis of the kind of passage which might confront you in an examination. Literary criticism is concerned with both the broader aspects of the work being studied and with its detail. The ideas which meet us in reading a great work of literature, and their relevance to us today, are an essential part of our study, and our Guides look at the thought of their subject in some detail. But just as essential is the craft with which the writer has constructed his work of art, and this may be considered under several technical headings – characterisation, language, style and stagecraft, for example.

The authors of these Guides are all teachers and writers of wide experience, and they have chosen to write about books they admire and know well in the belief that they can communicate their admiration to you. But you yourself must read and know intimately the book you are studying. No one can do that for you. You should see this book as a lamppost. Use it to shed light, not to lean against. If you know your text and know what it is saying about life, and how it says it, then you will enjoy it, and there is not better way of passing an examination in literature.

JAMES GIBSON

ACKNOWLEDGEMENTS

The author and publishers wish to thank the following who have kindly given permission for the use of copyright material: Oxford University Press for extracts from *The Works of Geoffrey Chaucer* 2nd edition, ed. F. N. Robinson, 1957.

All quotations from Chaucer are taken from F. N. Robinson (ed.), *The Works of Geoffrey Chaucer*, 2nd edition (Oxford University Press, 1957).

NOTE: Robinson treats the whole of Fragment 1 of the *Canterbury Tales* as a unit, so that in his text the first line of the *Knight's Tale* is numbered I 759.

Cover illustration: A detail from *The Ellesmere Manuscript, 1911 Facsimile: Beginning of the Knight's Tale*. Photograph © Shuckburgh Reynolds, London and by courtesy of the Bridgeman Art Library.

INTRODUCTION

In 1809 the poet William Blake wrote:

> Of Chaucer's characters, as described in his *Canterbury Tales*, some of the names or titles are altered by time, but the characters themselves for ever remain unaltered, and consequently they are the physiognomies or lineaments of universal human life, beyond which Nature never steps. Names alter, things never alter. I have known multitudes of those who would have been monks in the age of monkery, who in this deistical age are deists.

Even today, when we read the *General Prologue* to the *Canterbury Tales* it is easy to see what Blake meant. Although many of Chaucer's pilgrims have lost their occupations in the modern world their concerns, their behaviour and their mannerisms are still likely to strike us as familiar. It is tempting, and often instructive, to play the game, which Blake obviously played, of deciding on their places in our society.

We may visualise, for example, the Prioress, obsessed with appearances and with the forms of social behaviour, sentimental about small dogs, squeamish about mice, dispensing tea and delicately cut sandwiches in a dainty, rather over-cushioned drawing-room as she discusses the latest romantic novel. We might imagine, too, a modern equivalent of the Wife of Bath; rather loud, and strikingly, though not fashionably dressed; relentlessly sociable. We might give her her own – successful – business, and send her off a couple of times a year on expensive package holidays to conventionally exotic places in the sun. We might feel, too, that the Miller in his determination to turn himself into a human battering-ram has found his way onto the terraces of some of our football grounds – there isn't a door that he doesn't want to heave off its hinges, or break by running at it with his head.

With some of Chaucer's characters there is no need to play a transposition game at all since their occupations are still with us. The Merchant talks endlessly about his profits and sees the international situation in terms of its effects on his trade. His prosperous appearance, his display of expertise – Chaucer hints – are part of his stock in trade. His credit depends on his credibility, and no one knows whether or not he's in debt. The character is a familiar stereotype of the successful businessman; he is a stereotype we've encountered many times in modern novels or on television programmes.

Equally familiar is the Sergeant of the Law, that eminent lawyer, his activities described in lawyer's jargon in order to impress on us his skill in his profession. He is a man of the highest probity, or seems to be, extraordinarily busy and in demand – but not quite so busy as he seems. Again, the picture is one that has survived, and which we recognise quickly enough.

This shock of recognition across the centuries is part of what gives Chaucer life for us, and as we continue to read him and learn something of the time in which he lived we may be struck by many similarities between his world and ours. The Black Death, that plague which swept across Europe in 1348 and was to reappear at frequent intervals, had something of the same impact on people as nuclear weapons have had in our time, making them aware of the fragility of life, and of their own vulnerability. Like us, Chaucer lived in a time of rapid inflation and rising prices, of extremes of lavish spending and hardship. His was a time of social unrest and instability, when those who were successful or who supported the existing order deplored the changes they saw. Accounts of the Peasants' Revolt of 1381 echo uncannily some of the recent reactions to the inner city riots of our day. In Chaucer's poetry, and, indeed, in that of others of his contemporaries, there is a consciousness of the way in which different groups of people within their society hold different, often conflicting, values; a sense of a society at odds with itself. The labels conferred on the fourteenth century by modern historians are significant. It is a 'turbulent age', an 'age of adversity' an 'age of ambition'.

However, despite the parallels I have suggested between his age and ours, despite the immediacy of much of Chaucer's poetry, we need to be aware that to read Chaucer is to enter a world significantly different from ours; a world in which people behaved and organised themselves – even thought and felt – differently from us.

Many of these differences are probably best discussed at those points where they create difficulties for our understanding of the poetry. However, some account of Chaucer's life, and of the circles in which he moved, will provide a useful starting point for our study of the *Knight's Tale*.

1 CHAUCER AND THE ENGLISH COURT

1.1 CHAUCER

Chaucer was born around 1343 and died in 1400. He was a prolific poet with a high reputation among his contemporaries. He probably started work on that vastly ambitious project, the *Canterbury Tales*, quite late in his literary career, in the 1380s, and was still working on it at the time of his death. Before then he had produced a variety of works. He had translated into English two of the most influential texts in the later Middle Ages: the *Romance of the Rose*, a thirteenth-century French love allegory, and Boethius's *Consolation of Philosophy*, written in the sixth century when its author was facing execution. Chaucer had also written a number of great poems in English, including *Troilus and Criseyde*, one of the most moving love stories in our language. Although he wrote in English for an audience which considered French to be the fashionable language for poetry he was acclaimed as a great writer, and used as a model by a number of poets in the fifteenth and sixteenth centuries. Since then, important writers in every period have admired him, and many have felt him to be worth translating.

Yet Chaucer was not what we would call a professional poet. He was primarily a diplomat and civil servant, and most of the information we have about his life comes from official records and accounts books. He came from a family of prosperous merchants and moved in court circles for most of his life. His wife Philippa was in the Queen's service and was the sister of Katherine Swynford, mistress and, later, third wife of John of Gaunt, Edward III's fourth son, and one of the most powerful men in the country. Chaucer himself began his career as a page in the household of Elizabeth of Ulster, wife of Prince Lionel, the third son of Edward III, and moved into the King's household some time between 1360 and 1367.

After 1367, Chaucer travelled extensively in Europe on all kinds of business in the King's service; trade delegations, marriage negotiations, and on some secret missions. In 1374 he was appointed Controller of the Wool Custom and Subsidy, and was responsible for making sure that export duties on all the wool leaving the country were properly collected. His was an important position since the duties on wool made up a large part of the King's revenue. After the death of Edward III Chaucer was reappointed as Controller by Richard II and continued to hold the position until 1386 when the Parliament of that year, in which he himself sat, made determined efforts to overthrow the King's advisers. It seems that Chaucer was one of the casualties of the new dispensation. Although he gave up his position at the Wool Custom he remained Justice of the Peace for Kent, a position he held from 1385 to 1389. In 1389 Richard II made Chaucer his Clerk of the Works, another important position in which he was responsible for the building and maintenance of the King's properties. In 1391 Chaucer retired from the royal service.

Although this bald summary may seem to provide some bearings on Chaucer's life, its familar words conceal, in fact, almost as much as they reveal. 'Poet', 'poetry', 'King', 'Court', for example, are words which need further definition, for the fourteenth-century realities to which they refer are in many ways alien to our twentieth-century experience.

1.2 KING, COURT AND GOVERNMENT

To move in court circles, as Chaucer did, and to be the King's servant, was to be close to the centre of power, for the government of the realm rested in the King's hands and the country's stability and prosperity depended very largely upon his character. Although he ruled with the help of a council, the King appointed his own councillors and decided foreign policy, and those in charge of administering his law were responsible to him. However, the King's was a power hedged in by insecurity and danger for within their own territories the magnates, the great lords who were often related to the King, exercised a control which almost equalled his, and could raise forces to rebel against him. Two kings in the fourteenth century, Edward II in 1327 and Richard II in 1399, were deposed and murdered, and a number of their most valued servants came to grief with them.

Chaucer served both Edward III (the son of Edward II) and

Richard II, and in his lifetime the power of the Crown was weakened considerably.

Conscious, perhaps, of his father's fate, but also because he shared many of their concerns and values, Edward gave his magnates more share in government, increasing their representation on his council to outweigh that of his chosen administrators and justices and taking care not to appoint anyone who lacked their support. By the reign of Richard II the magnates had established their right to give advice on all important matters, and the King's Council was on the way to becoming a Parliament in something of the modern sense. Representatives of the boroughs and the counties (Knights of the Shire), too, came to have some influence. Because Edward needed their cooperation in raising money for the Hundred Years' War against France they gained the right to control taxation, and to petition the King about their grievances. Towards the end of the century they had come to be regarded as a part of Parliament along with the magnates, though their actual power was very limited. While they might have the right to petition the king, for example, the king was under no obligation to grant their wishes.

The magnates had increased in power but they were not always – or indeed often – in agreement with one another, and during the last years of Edward III's reign, when the King was too ill and senile to govern, there were bitter struggles between various factions among them.

In 1377 at the age of ten, Richard II came to the throne of a country unsuccessful in war and full of internal discontent. 'Woe to the land where the King is a boy' was a popular saying of the time, and Richard's minority was marked by in-fighting among members of the council which had been appointed to govern for him. As Richard grew older he tried to throw off the power of the council and to reassert royal authority by exploiting these factions, but in 1386 he was forced by a group of powerful magnates to dismiss the ministers he had appointed, and a couple of years later, after his forces had been defeated, many of his supporters were executed and imprisoned.

For the rest of his reign Richard worked steadily at restoring the royal power, and those who rebelled against him in 1388 were eventually accused of treason and executed. Richard finally overreached himself, however, in his attempt to curb the powerful house of Lancaster, when he condemned Henry, the eldest son of John of Gaunt, to permanent exile and debarred him from his inheritance. Rebellion followed almost immediately, and in 1399 Richard was deposed (though a fiction that he had abdicated was maintained). He was murdered soon after.

Although it was imperative for the King to take into account the interests and customary rights of his magnates, no one questioned his theoretical right to govern his country. Legal pretexts, backed by force, might be found to remove unsatisfactory kings, but the King was still the centre of government, and because of this his Court was an important physical centre. The Court was where the King was, and it was there that policies were discussed; there that men could seek office, advance their interests and gain promotion; there that they could use their influence. Chaucer, then, because of his position at Court, was brought into close touch – sometimes too close, one might suspect – with the political realities of his day in all their instability and danger. Perhaps because of this, we find in his best poetry a sense of the way in which individual lives are affected and even dominated by events taking place in their society.

1.3 COURTLY CULTURE

As well as being the centre of government the Court was also a centre of culture and the arts; a milieu in which an aristocratic life-style found its fullest expression, and where the aristocratic values attributed to Chaucer's Knight – 'trouthe and honour, fredom and curteisie' – were paid tribute to, though it must be admitted that neither Edward III or Richard II were noted for their *trouthe* if the word is taken in its narrowest sense of promise-keeping.

Although the Courts of both Edward and Richard were centres of culture and of luxury each had a different ethos. Where Edward III shared the tastes of his barons for jousting and tournaments and entered into the entertainments of the Court with an easy informality, Richard might be said to be obsessed with style. Cooking became an art in his household and elaborate and exotic banquets were prepared for him (his cookery book still exists); sumptuous and heavily bejewelled clothes, particularly for men, echoed his taste in dress (Chaucer's Squire is embroidered like a meadow, all in fresh flowers . . .) and the arts, both visual and literary, flourished. If, as has been claimed, *fredom* (an open-handed generosity and informality) was Edward's primary value, Richard's was, perhaps, *honour* in the sense in which the word is used in the *Knight's Tale* – ceremonious behaviour befitting one's rank, or showing someone the deference due to his position.

In 1382 Richard married Anne of Bohemia, the daughter of the Holy Roman Emperor, and it may be that her influence was at least partially responsible for the formality and sophistication of Richard's court. Certainly Richard's tastes were European rather than English, and he looked towards the continent for new fashions in dress, art and literature. In such an environment living itself became something of an art form, and social accomplishments and exquisite manners were prized.

Two of Chaucer's pilgrims seem to embody, or to aspire to, ideal courtly behaviour. The Squire is young, fashionably dressed, a good horseman. He can dance well and sing, play musical instruments and compose songs and poetry. The Prioress tries very hard; she takes pains to imitate courtly manners, to behave with dignity, and wants to be treated with deference. Chaucer spends some time in describing her careful, rather finicking table manners, commenting somewhat wryly that she delighted in courtesy. In this particular context the meaning of the word *curteisie* is narrowed to not much more than upper class etiquette (and we may remember that Richard II introduced the use of the handkerchief). The Squire, too is described as *curteis*, and the example of his courtesy that we are given is that he 'carf biforn his fader at the table'. He played his part, with fitting deference (he was respectful and made himself useful too), in the life of a noble household in which mealtimes were an occasion for ceremony.

1.4 COURTLY LOVE

Both the Squire and the Prioress have another preoccupation: love. This, too, is a part of their courtliness or, in the case of the latter, her aspiration to be courtly.

Love, courtly love or *fin amor* is one of the great themes of later medieval literature, and one which has affected European culture even down to our own times. Strange as it may seem to us, medieval poets before the twelfth century showed comparatively little interest in the love between men and women. On the whole, secular poetry preferred to deal with heroic exploits; its stories were of bravery, loyalty and endurance. In twelfth-century Provence, however, a fashion for love poetry began, and spread throughout western Europe. This fashion has, of course, never died, and the stereotypical heroines of our romantic novels and films are the distant descendants of the courtly ladies of medieval romances. Some of our ways, too, of thinking about love, and the language we use to describe it, have their roots in that remote past, did not really exist before then, and are not be found in other cultures. Although the behaviour of the lovers in the *Knight's Tale* may strike the modern reader as extreme, or even ludicrous, the language they use of love, and the assumptions that language expresses, are not alien to us.

The literature of love was highly conventional, as conventional as much of the popular literature of our day, and certain features recur with remarkable regularity in medieval romances and books about love. The characters are almost without exception of noble birth, the heroine is usually blonde (as I said, little has changed), with grey eyes, red lips and a high forehead. She is slender, but nicely rounded; friendly but modest, not to say distant. Her lover, overwhelmed by her beauty, does not dare to approach her at first, or to reveal his love to any but a trustworthy friend. When he at last speaks his advances are usually rejected (instant acceptance might raise doubts about the lady's virtue), but he is completely within his lady's *daunger*, her control. Originally *daunger* was the power a feudal lord exerted over his knights, but the word used metaphorically in love literature, and extended its meaning to include 'scorn'. It is, as you may have guessed, the ancestor of our word 'danger'. Once in his lady's *daunger* the lover was prepared to serve her indefinitely in the hope that he would one day win her love. The words used of the lady's love: 'mercy', 'pity', 'grace' suggest the lover's helplessness and subservience to her. Unlike modern romances the successful love affair did not always, or indeed usually, end in marriage, though marriage was a more common outcome in English romances than in French ones. Since marriage was so much a matter of business negotiations between families it was seen, in literature at least, as having nothing to do with love, and love relationships were frequently adulterous. The most famous in literature is probably that of Lancelot and Guinivere.

Much of the literature I have described was written purely for entertainment, but in some works the question of love is treated with great seriousness, and the love between men and women is portrayed as ennobling, a moral force which gives the lovers' lives depth and meaning.

Inevitably, this interest in love did not stay enclosed within the pages of books; the manners and attitudes of individuals were shaped variously by it. At the most trivial level, a kind of formalised flirtation seems to have been part of polite conversation, romantic friendships between men and women were common, and more significantly the language and attitudes of love literature provided a means by which individuals could express their deepest feelings. Thus, although

Richard II's marriage to Anne of Bohemia had been arranged for political reasons, the affection which grew between them seems to have been conceived by Richard in the terms of courtly love. On Anne's death he burned down, in the ultimate courtly gesture, his palace at Sheen with its Royal Lodging where she had died.

1.5 POETRY

In an environment where so much emphasis was placed on social accomplishments, and on elegant and refined living, entertainment was obviously important, and as well as dancing and games of various kinds, poetry was regarded as a diversion. At one time minstrels had been employed in great households to entertain the guests at banquets. These men had been skilled in their craft, skilled in recounting and recasting stories, but they were paid employees and regarded as social inferiors. By the end of the fourteenth century, however, although minstrels were still employed in great households, the word 'minstrel' had come to have something of its modern meaning and was used generally of musicians. Poets, tellers of stories, operated more as amateurs, and to be able to write poetry was seen as a social accomplishment even amongst the most noble. Thus, Chaucer's Squire, that model of elegance 'koude songes make and wel endite', and the young squire, Aurelius, in the *Franklin's Tale* expresses his love for the heroine Dorigen in a variety of verse forms – lays, songs, complaints, roundels, virelays. Such poems were probably read aloud, passed around, set to music.

Even those who took their craft seriously and produced more than passing entertainment were not professional poets in the way we would understand the term. Their work might produce incidental rewards; bring them gifts, or even a pension, or some kind of sinecure, but it was not seen as a full-time occupation. John Lydgate, Chaucer's younger contemporary, was a monk, and John Gower, a man of good family, to whom Chaucer dedicated *Troilus and Criseyde*, lived for much of the later part of his life in a religious house.

Chaucer, Gower and Lydgate were prolific writers and in fact produced more works than many later poets, and that their poetry provided them with little income is to do with the conditions under which literature was produced and transmitted in their time.

We have to remember that they lived before the invention of the printing press. In their day every single copy of a work had to be written out by hand, either by the person who wanted it, or by a professional scribe. If one thinks of the *Canterbury Tales* with its twenty-four stories, its *General Prologue* and the connecting passages between tales one can gain some sense of what this method of reproduction meant for the circulation of books.

By our standards there were very few books; works were borrowed by friends to be copied, or read aloud to small or large groups. Indeed the very idea of a book has altered since then. We tend to think of a book as being a single work or, in the case of poetry, a group of works that are related in some way; either by author or period or theme. In the Middle Ages it was common for individuals who had collected manuscripts to have them all bound together, almost regardless of their contents, into one large volume. When we read of someone possessing eight, or ten, or twenty books we do not really know how many books, in our sense of the word, this amounted to unless we have a list of contents.

Because of the way in which books were produced they were not only less standardised but much more highly prized as physical objects. Those possessed by the King and the very rich were often objects of great beauty, wonderfully copied and lavishly illustrated in glowing colours. These manuscripts *de luxe* were works of art, and beyond the means of any save the wealthy.

In such a situation it is easy to understand why there were few professional poets. A poet might be commissioned to produce a particular work for a wealthy patron, or even for a bookseller, but after that there would be no royalties, and any profits would go to the producers and sellers of manuscripts. However, poets dedicated, and often presented, their works to the King or to some great magnate in the hope of reward. It is likely that some of the pensions and perquisites Chaucer received were such rewards. Near the end of his life Chaucer wrote a ruefully comic poem, 'The Complaint of Chaucer to his Purse', to the new King, Henry IV, asking for help in his financial predicament

> To yow, my purse, and to noon other wight
> Complayne I, for ye be my lady dere!
> I am so sory, now that ye ben lyght;
> For certes, but ye make me hevy chere.

After continuing for another couple of stanzas to address his purse as his not altogether satisfactory lady, Chaucer turns his attention to the king, concluding on a note of extravagant and hopeful flattery

> O conquerour of Brutes Albyon,
>
> . . .
>
> Have mynde upon my supplicacion!

In Chaucer's time, the very idea of a poet was different from ours, which has grown out of both technological changes and changes in the way we value the individual. After the coming of printing in the late fifteenth century writers *very* gradually (the process took several centuries) were able to free themselves from their dependence on patrons and to live from the profits of their work. Writers thus came to have a professional, independent status. Gradually, too, individual perceptions came to have a very high value placed upon them and the individual came to be seen as in opposition to, rather than a part of, society. The triumph of individualism came with the Romantic movement, and it is largely because of the writings of the Romantics that we have become accustomed to think of poets as somewhat set apart, to think of great poets as discovering and revealing to us truths about our condition. Shelley's claim that 'poets are the un-acknowledged legislators of the world' is probably one that most of us pay lip service to without ever really thinking about it. If we think he pitched his claim too high, then we probably still have a stereotypical figure of a poet as someone unworldly, rather out of the mainstream of life, and preoccupied with his own feelings and perceptions. Post-Romantic, too, is our assumption that originality is a value in serious writing. If we want to praise a writer we say his work is new, or fresh, or experimental.

In the Middle Ages men had rather different values. Society was hierarchical, undemocratic. Power was conferred by God on its rulers who, in turn, imposed that power (whatever the restrictions defined by custom) on those below them. The proper function of the individual was to act in accordance with his place in society.

In such a hierarchical society authority was a value no less in the world of the mind than in the material world, and it would have been considered presumptuous to assert one's own views in opposition to the great writers of the past, upon whom time had conferred authority. *These* were the *auctors* (literally authorities); poets of the present were not *auctors* but 'makers', at their most serious, trans-mitters of the wisdom of their *auctors*. 'As myn auctor seyth' is the way in which a medieval writer claims respectful attention for his words.

However, this stark and over-simple contrast between then and now needs some qualification, for during the fourteenth century, just as there was a tendency for religion to become more private and introspective than it had been formerly, so some of the major poets moved towards finding a more personal voice. They did not set themselves up against their *auctors*, but made use of such literary forms as the dream vision (for dreams could, after all, be a source of authoritative revelation) to express their sense of the world. One of the most questioning – and one of the most popular – poems of the period, *Piers Plowman*, takes the form of a series of dreams in which its narrator attempts to make sense of a society full of suffering and evil. Chaucer himself made use of the dream form frequently in his early poems, adopting in them the stance of a naïve, wondering dreamer, not too dissimilar from the pilgrim-narrator of the *Canterbury Tales*. Within his use of his *auctors*, too, Chaucer finds space to express his own sense of things, often slyly questioning the authority he presents for our acceptance, sometimes placing contradictory authorities side by side, sometimes even inventing them.

Even at their most individual, however, medieval poets on the whole contented themselves with giving a new slant to old stories. They did not present their own experience directly as a standard for their readers or assume that their readers would be interested in the detail of their lives, as Wordsworth did when he wrote *The Prelude*. Anything apart from a spiritual autobiography would have been regarded as presumptuous.

1.6 CHAUCER'S LANGUAGE

The seventeenth-century poet, Dryden, called Chaucer 'the father of English poetry', and this description has something of a literal truth about it. Although there were other poets writing in English before and contemporary with Chaucer, the language of those not directly influenced by him is much further away from ours than his; their styles, themes and subject matter on the whole outside the English tradition as it developed under his influence. Those works, too, seem to have been less popular than Chaucer's in his own time, perhaps because they were provincial, and of many of them few or even no copies remain.

To notice that Chaucer has few antecedents in English takes us into another area in which fourteenth-century England was different from the present day; that of the languages people spoke and read. Latin was the language of the Church, and the language of learning. Indeed, most learning was in the hands of the Church and able scholars at the universities were more than likely to progress to a study of theology after they had studied arts subjects. That Latin was the language of learning meant that scholars all over Europe could communicate easily with one another and could go – much more frequently than now – to the different centres of learning that had grown up all over Europe. It meant also that scholars, much more obviously than now, shared a common culture, particularly since quite a small number of texts was regarded as central to the various disciplines.

After Latin, French enjoyed a high status in England, for ever since the Norman Conquest in 1066 French had been the language of legal transactions (though by the fourteenth century this was changing), of most literature and of polite conversation among the nobility. By Chaucer's time, and probably considerably earlier, English was the first language of nearly everyone, but speaking French was a mark of one's social status – rather in the way some accents are today – and anyone with social pretensions would be able to do so, and to enjoy French literature. You may remember that Chaucer's Prioress, that indefatigable pursuer of courtly accomplishments, speaks French very well, even if she does so with a London accent.

We have, then, a society in which many people, and nearly all the nobility have some grasp of at least three languages. Some are trilingual. John Gower wrote one of his three major works in Latin, another in English, and a third in French, and Chaucer translated both Latin and French (and, indeed, Italian) works.

Although nationalism was coming to be a force in men's lives, and, to alter their attitude to the languages they used, the Court, particularly under Richard II, looked to Europe for marriage alliances and for its culture. Under these circumstances it is more remarkable that a poet like Chaucer, writing for the court, and one who took his poetry seriously, should have written in English than that he should have had few predecessors. Remarkable, too, that his poetry, written in such a low-status language, should have been valued so highly. Perhaps the explanation lies in his novelty in a Court obsessed with fashion. Chaucer's journeys abroad brought him into close contact with the great writers of the continent, and his assimilation of their fashions into his own language may have added that extra twist of newness which would have appealed to those around Richard.

It is, therefore, important to recognise that although Chaucer wrote in English, his verse forms, stylistic models and sources are predominantly Continental. In his early work the French influence is most strong, but Italy, with its three great writers, Dante, Petrarch and Boccaccio, is the dominating inspiration of his best work (I shall discuss in detail Chaucer's use of Boccaccio in the *Knight's Tale* in 5).

It may be that Chaucer came in touch with the Italian language and its poetry in his dealings as Controller of Customs with Italian merchants. Certainly, his diplomatic missions took him to Italy on a number of occasions, perhaps as early as 1368 for the marriage of Prince Lionel to Violante, the daughter of Galeazzo Visconti of Milan, certainly in 1372–3 when he visited Genoa and Florence, the birthplace of Dante, on a trade mission. Another set of marriage negotiations took him back to Italy in 1378. These visits would probably have given him the opportunity to visit libraries containing the works of Dante, Petrarch and Boccaccio, and perhaps to have some of their manuscripts copied. His own poetry shows an intimate knowledge of some of the works of all three poets. The *Clerk's Tale* is a close translation of a work by Petrarch, Dante is quoted in the *Wife of Bath's Tale* and Boccaccio plundered and adapted in the *Knight's Tale* and in *Troilus and Criseyde*. Chaucer was a European poet, and he helped to transform English from a provincial dialect into a language capable of expressing the most philosophical and subtle ideas. It was not for nothing that the French poet Eustache Deschamps heaped rather fulsome praise on him, comparing him with the great *auctors* of the past (the highest accolade). Significantly, Deschamps ends every verse of his poem with the refrain 'Great translator, Geoffrey Chaucer.'

2 THE *CANTERBURY TALES*

2.1 THE TEXT

It is as well to remember that the version of the *Knight's Tale* which you have in your modern edition does not look precisely like any of the versions in the various manuscripts still in existence. Nor does it present exactly what its author wrote.

Up to a point this is true of all editions of medieval, and even later, works. At the most basic level conventions of transcription have changed. For instance, in the fourteenth century there were letters in the alphabet which have now gone out of use. This does not really cause problems, for we can express the sounds they represent by combinations of the letters we use.

More importantly, punctuation has changed too. Medieval works are very lightly punctuated, so the punctuation in your edition of the *Knight's Tale* has been added by its editor. Punctuation, however, is a part of the way in which we convey meaning and adding a full stop, choosing to use a comma instead of a colon, adding speech marks, can influence the sense of a passage quite significantly. Notice how different ways of punctuating the following lines from the *General Prologue* produce different meanings:

> And whan he rood, men myghte his brydel heere
> Gynglen in a whistlynge wynd als cleere
> And eek as loude as dooth the chapel belle.
> Ther as this lord was kepere of the celle . . .

and:

> as loude as dooth the chapel belle
> Ther as this lord was kepere of the celle

If there is no full stop placed after 'belle' then we are told that the sound of his bridle is louder than his *own* chapel bell, not just any chapel bell, and the implied criticism seems to be stronger. To punctuate a work is to interpret as well as to clarify a writer's meaning, and to do that is to impose as well as to expose meaning.

These are fairly minor matters, though. More serious difficulties arise when we try to recapture a medieval writer's exact words. These have to do with the way in which works were reproduced. In the days before printing every copy of a work had to be transcribed laboriously by hand. If you have ever tried to copy even short passages of someone else's writing you will have some idea of the ease with which mistakes could be made, even by a highly practised scribe. In copying a long, handwritten text it is easy for the eye to jump lines, easy to substitute a more familar word for a less, to transpose letters, and so on. Unless editors can be sure that they have the author's own copy they have to engage in highly complicated detective work, sometimes by comparing different manuscripts of the same work where these are available, sometimes by deducing from their knowledge of common mistakes what the author is likely to have written.

Any editor of the *Canterbury Tales* faces additional problems for so far as we can tell the work was unfinished when Chaucer died. We possess no complete version, but only fragments of it. There is a clearly defined beginning in which the pilgrim-narrator describes most of the pilgrims he meets at the Tabard Inn at Southwark. Like him they are preparing to visit the shrine of Thomas à Becket at Canterbury. Outlined in the *General Prologue* there is what may be a plan for the whole work. Harry Bailly, the Host of the Tabard, suggests that each pilgrim should tell two stories on the way to Canterbury, and two on the way back; they will stand the teller of the best tale a dinner, and he will ride with the pilgrims to adjudicate and see fair play.

After the General Prologue there is a group of tales which are connected with it and with one another by means of short passages containing exchanges between the pilgrims. This is followed by other fragments of the whole work containing groups of tales similarly linked. Some of the tales are unfinished, not all the pilgrims have tales, and there are less than a quarter of the number suggested by the Host. However, the work seems to have a clearly defined ending. The last tale – a sermon on sin and penitence – is told by the Parson as the company comes within sight of Canterbury, and the work ends with a retraction by Chaucer, this time speaking in his own voice, of all those of his works which might be considered sinful. However, to end the work with the arrival of the pilgrims at Canterbury does not agree with the Host's plan in the *General Prologue*. It may be that Chaucer changed his mind about the number of tales the work was to contain, or even that the Host's programme was never intended as a plan for the author. We shall never know. Scholars continue to discuss what the *Canterbury Tales* might have looked like had Chaucer lived to complete them; how what is in existence should be arranged, and even whether Chaucer wrote all of it.

There are over eighty manuscripts of the *Canterbury Tales* in various states of completeness or preservation. All of them were produced after Chaucer's death, some a long time after. Most of them are copies, or copies of copies, of the two earliest, the Ellesmere and Hengwrt manuscripts. Both of these were produced between 1400 and 1410 and were probably copied by the same scribe. However, they are very different in a number of ways; so much so that our reading of the *Canterbury Tales* is likely to be influenced by our decision as to which represents Chaucer's original most faithfully. The arguments for preferring one manuscript over another are complex, and I cannot hope to do justice to them within the scope of this book, but I shall outline them briefly so that you will be able to understand some of the uncertainties surrounding the text.

Ellesmere is a *de luxe* manuscript, beautifully copied, and illustrated with pictures of the pilgrims. It is very carefully laid out, as though the scribe had all his material around him and was therefore able to arrange it properly and to plan how his finished work would look. The manuscript has headings and titles which assign the various tales to their tellers; it has also more linking passages between its tales than Hengwrt, as well as a tale with its own long prologue which are both missing from Hengwrt, the *Canon's Yeoman's Prologue* and *Tale*. It arranges the tales in a different order, too.

Hengwrt is much less elegant than Ellesmere. There are gaps between various tales as though the scribe has left room to insert material, and the way in which the leaves of the manuscript are put together suggests that some of the material was rearranged, either while the work was in the process of being copied or after it had been substantially finished. The different colours of the inks used in the manuscripts suggest, too, that spaces were left for some passages which were added later. Like Ellesmere, Hengwrt has running titles (titles at the top of pages, and not just at the beginning of chapters) but these have been added by a different scribe some time after the manuscript was produced. Generally speaking, Hengwrt seems to reproduce more accurately than Ellesmere Chaucer's actual words.

In what way do the differences between the two manuscripts affect our reading of the work? Quite simply, Ellesmere's arrangement and the extra material it contains bind the tales both to their tellers and to one another more closely. The pictures at the beginning of each tale emphasise the relation of tale to teller, and the additional exchanges between the different pilgrims keep before our minds more forcibly the ground fiction of the pilgrimage to Canterbury (though it must be stressed that most such exchanges occur in Hengwrt too). The fiction of the journey is also emphasised by the sudden arrival of two new pilgrims, the Canon and his Yeoman, who ride up to join the existing company. Although Ellesmere does not put in their proper order the various places on the route to Canterbury which are mentioned in the text, it nevertheless gives us a work which seems to be a unified whole, despite its unfinishedness. Hengwrt, by contrast, presents us with a collection of tales which are more loosely connected, and in which the characters of the pilgrims seem slightly less important.

How do we decide which of the two works represents Chaucer's plans more closely? Those who claim that Hengwrt is the more reliable version remind us that it reproduces Chaucer's actual words more accurately, and point out that the ordering, the titles and the headings of Ellesmere are the work of an editor. It has also been claimed that since the same scribe produced both manuscripts the more disordered Hengwrt must be the earlier of the two, and represent a first attempt at ordering Chaucer's drafts. If it is assumed that the scribe who produced Hengwrt had all of Chaucer's papers available, then those linking passages for which space was left as the scribe was copying must be spurious, since they would have been composed after Chaucer's death. On this assumption the *Canon's Yeoman's Prologue* and *Tale* must be spurious too since they do not appear in Hengwrt.

The weakness in this argument, of course, is that it depends absolutely on the assumption that the scribe of Hengwrt *did* have all the various portions of the *Canterbury Tales* in front of him when he began copying, *and* that they were arranged in such a way that he was able to copy what he had consecutively. It is quite possible, however, that the *Canon's Yeoman's Prologue* and *Tale* had been loaned to someone and became available only later; possible, too, that the scribe knew that some linking passages existed, either among the papers he had in front of him, or in a more complete version of portions of the work, and left room to add them when he could get hold of them. Our real difficulty is that we have absolutely no evidence concerning the state of the *Canterbury Tales* on Chaucer's death except the words of the text and the appearance of the manuscripts.

In my reading of the *Canterbury Tales* I take Ellesmere in its

contents and broad outline as being closer to Chaucer's plan than
Hengwrt. Even if we accept that its arrangement is that of an editor
there is nothing in that arrangement which distorts in any way what
the text tells us. Moreover, the arguments for rejecting the material
not in Hengwrt, and indeed some of the passages in it, ignore their
quality. It is hard to imagine that there was another poet – unknown
to us – writing in that period who was sufficiently skilful to have
imitated Chaucer's style so well, particuarly in such a long work as
the *Canon's Yeoman's Prologue* and *Tale*. My reading, then, takes
the *Canterbury Tales* as a single work, and assumes that in order to
understand its parts properly we have to set them in the context of the
whole.

2.2 THE GENERAL PROLOGUE

In the *General Prologue* the organising fiction of the journey to
Canterbury on which the pilgrims will tell their stories is established
with great vividness. The *Prologue* opens with a formal, rhetorical
description of the awakening of new life in the spring. The passage is
eighteen lines long, and shaped into one carefully organised sentence
which, with its 'When . . . Then . . . ' construction, seems to impli-
cate the human urge to go on pilgrimage with the seasonal stirrings of
activity in the natural world:

> Whan that Aprill with his shoures soote
> The droghte of March hath perced to the roote . . .
> Thanne longen folk to goon on pilgrimages

After this beautiful, formal opening the narrator drops into a chatty
tone, and we are taken from a contemplation of the patterns of
nature into a close-up of an inn in Southwark where one group of
pilgrims is preparing for the journey.

In what follows we are given a vivid description of most of the
pilgrims who will be our story-tellers; we learn in varying amounts of
detail about their physical appearance, their clothes, their horses,
their day to day activities. Sometimes the accents of their speech
seem to drown those of the narrator as he reports their words:

> What sholde he studie and make hymselven wood,
> Upon a book in cloystre alwey to poure,
> Or swynken with his handes, and laboure,
> As Austyn bit? How shal the world be served?
> Lat Austyn have his swynk to hym reserved!

Part of what makes the characters seem so lifelike is the variety of ways in which they are described, for Chaucer follows no set plan and accentuates sometimes one aspect of character, now another. Sometimes he seems to know everything about the character he has created, at others he is reduced to guessing. One feature alone remains constant: just as the characters are labelled by their occupations, so their skill in those occupations is always emphasised (this is true even of the Wife of Bath, for 'woman' or 'wife' was then a description of occupation – rather as 'housewife' can be, even now, on some kinds of official form). His pilgrims, Chaucer stresses (often using ironically the same terms to praise quite different qualities) are all extremely good at their jobs; the Knight is 'a verray, parfit gentil knyght', the Physician 'a verray, parfit praktisour', and however repellent the Pardoner might be as a man

> of his craft, fro Berwyk into Ware
> Ne was ther swich another pardoner.

The pilgrims are not only outstanding at their jobs, they are almost a cross-section of their society; only the very lowly and the very powerful are not represented. Moreover, they are sometimes arranged in such a way as to suggest a connection between the members of the different groups. It seems fitting that the eminent lawyer should ride with the Franklin who, if not aristocratic, is a land holder and a powerful figure in his area; A Justice of the Peace, a Member of Parliament.

Sometimes the characters are connected with one another, not by their shared interests, but by the way in which others value them. The Summoner and the Pardoner ride together in tipsy companionship; parodies of God's justice and His mercy. Their occupations do not suggest a friendship between them as likely, but their association underlines the common opinion that members of both professions are crooks.

Much has been written – and with justification – about the realism of the *General Prologue*, but it is important to recognise that this realism grows out of convention (indeed, it is questionable whether realism ever arises from *direct* observation of life). The *Prologue* belongs to the genre of estates satire, a type of literature popular in the Middle Ages. In such satire the characteristic failings of members of different occupations are described and mocked. Estates satire created and perpetuated social stereotypes; Friars were money-grabbing and lecherous, Monks lecherous, Millers thieving, and so on.

However, although Chaucer gives his characters the failings habitually associated with them, his criticism of his society is more penetrating and fundamental than that usually found in estates satire. Implicit in traditional estates satire is the assumption that the ideal society is made up of mutually supporting groups. The underlying, and very powerful, model is that of three broad groups or 'estates'; those who fight and govern, those who pray and teach, and those who till the land. The knight protects other members of his society, the priest prays for and teaches them, and the peasant provides food, the means of physical life, for all.

In the *General Prologue* this model of the three estates is called to the reader's mind by the figures of Knight, Parson and Plowman. All appear to be praised without reservation and to be exemplary members of their groups. However, in all three portraits there is that which perhaps creates a sense of unease: the Knight's prowess in fighting seems to have little to do with any defence of the land; the Parson is zealous in his fulfilment of his duties, but many of his activities are couched in negative terms – he doesn't leave his flock in order to find extra employment, he doesn't stay at home because of bad weather, he doesn't excommunicate people for not paying their tithes – at the very least, there is a strong implication that he is exceptional; we may also feel his virtues, expressed so negatively, to be rather less than attractive. The third figure, the Plowman, by contrast with the other vivid, if imperfect, characters of the *Prologue*, is shadowy; an ideal without an identity.

Moreover, while the model of the three estates may be suggested, the *General Prologue* is likely to impress on us that its characters rely for their prosperity on competition rather than on mutual support. Many of the characters are so successful at their jobs because they can strike a hard bargain, because they can exploit the needs of their fellows, often with some trickery, it is hinted. Their moral failings are thus presented to us as essential to their professional success.

Chaucer emphasises also, in the case of some characters, the way in which the groups to which they belong have importances which contradict, or at least sit uneasily with, the expressed ideals of those groups. The Monk's worldly interests and physical impressiveness seem strange qualifications for a position of responsibility in an institution vowed to austerity and service to God. and yet, we are told, he is 'A manly man, to been an abbot able'.

Chaucer seems to show us in a variety of ways, a set of individuals who, while they are less than perfect, are yet perfect – that is, perfectly typical – representatives of their professions. We may come to feel then that the society he describes is one in which there is no shared ideal of community, but rather a collection of groups, some of which may be united at the expense of others, but all of which pursue their own ends in defiance of any common good.

Because he presents his characters as being so successful in their occupations the estates ideal which Chaucer has called to our minds thus seems to be inadequate to describe or control a complicated society in which the pursuit of wealth and status erode any idea of hierarchy.

How *un*hierarchical this society is emerges clearly at the end of the *Prologue* when the narrator asks the forgiveness of his audience for not arranging his pilgrims according to their rank. 'My wit is short, ye may wel understonde.' he says by way of excuse. But can we, the audience, arrange this group in any better order?

2.3 **THE NARRATION OF THE** *CANTERBURY TALES*

In this society of conflicting interests which Chaucer creates we are made to feel the difficulty of finding shared values, and of judging by any authoritative standard the different perceptions of the world which its characters reveal. Chaucer confronts us with this difficulty, not only in *what* he describes to us, but in the very form which that description takes.

It is important to recognise that in the *General Prologue* Chaucer does not speak to his audience as an author who is on a different level from his characters, standing above them and knowing everything about them. The voice we hear is that of a pilgrim, someone who has met, and is riding with, the company he describes. What he tells us purports to be what he has observed. But if the pilgrimage and the pilgrims are a fiction, then so too the pilgrim-narrator is a fictional character; the judgements he makes are those of someone who is a part of the story. This means that we cannot assume that they are Chaucer's judgements and have a special authority. That is, we are not given a perspective from outside the work which we can adopt (compare the way in which writers like Jane Austen or George Eliot tell us authoritatively what to think of their characters).

Moreover, this pilgrim-narrator of Chaucer's is likely to strike us as rather unreliable. He doesn't always know everything about the characters he describes, his praise of them is all-embracing, and he describes with admiration activities which surely ought to be condemned. His worry, too, at the end of the *General Prologue*, when he realises that some of the stories he is about to repeat might offend his audience has a tone of comic helplessness about it.

At the same time, as the work goes on we are encouraged to connect this narrator with Chaucer the poet. The Man of Law in his prologue describes rather disparagingly all the poems Chaucer has written, and when it is the narrator's turn to tell a story his incompetence develops into a kind of joke. The Host very quickly stops his attempts at verse; 'The drasty rymyng is nat worth a toord!' he exclaims, and suggests that he might find prose easier. Chaucer, then, seems to dethrone himself as author, as authority by his very method of narration, and seems to be saying, 'My judgement is no better than that of my characters. My way of seeing the world is one among many'. We as readers thus become implicated in the world of conflicting standards he presents, and are unable to accept the viewpoint of any one tale as clearly authoritative – however *un*-authoritative those of some tales are.

2.4 CHARACTERISATION OF THE PILGRIMS

The variety of ways in which Chaucer presents his pilgrims enforces, too, a realisation of the limits of individual perception. In the *General Prologue* the description of the characters focuses strongly upon how they appear to others. We are told what they look like, how they behave and the kind of reputation they have. Any inferences about their personalities are of the kind we make about people we meet. Although we sometimes seem to hear their voices, we are not taken into their thoughts.

As the work progresses we see some of the pilgrims in action, quarrelling or forming alliances among themselves, and many of them are given an opportunity to reveal themselves – occasionally at length – in their prologues to their tales. The Pardoner, the Wife of Bath, the Canon's Yeoman produce something in the nature of autobiography, revealing themselves from the inside. Even in some of the quite short prologues we are given glimpses of an internal world which sometimes gives a new and rather surprising perspective on what we already know.

The tales which the pilgrims tell are yet another way of revealing them as characters, for their stories establish their values and their importances; sometimes their fantasies. Some tales seem to exist, indeed, less as tales than as exhibitions of character.

The connections between these different aspects of the pilgrims' characters are sometimes made for us; for example we are told in the *General Prologue* that the Wife of Bath is rather deaf; in her own prologue we find out why. Sometimes there seem to be inconsistencies between external description, autobiography and tale, and then we find ourselves engaged in inventing connections, just as in real life we try to account for inconsistencies in the behaviour of the people we know, or try to understand why they should be described differently by different people.

2.5 PILGRIMAGE

The fiction of the pilgrimage is a realistic device for bringing together such an unlikely assortment of characters as we find in the *Canterbury Tales*, for pilgrimages were an important feature of medieval life. Great pilgrim routes stretched across Europe and to the Holy Land, leading to the shrines of saints and to sacred places. Along such routes were inns and shelters for pilgrims. Along the routes, too, it was easy in the interests of safety to join other travellers and journey in large companies. To some extent, pilgrimage was rather like modern tourism. Shrines attracted visitors, and brought money and prestige to those in charge of them, so that there was often competition among various religious houses to acquire the relics of important saints.

Clearly the motives of many pilgrims were not unmixedly devout; pilgrimage could be a way of seeing the world, or even of avoiding trouble at home; wealthy men who had had pilgrimage imposed on them as a penance sometimes paid one of their followers to make the journey for them. Thus, pilgrimage was treated with some suspicion in the writing of the times.

However, in an age when belief in God and in the power of his saints to intercede for men was as natural as the modern assumption that the world is round, the idea of pilgrimage was powerful. To visit the shrine of a saint was to come into close contact with his or her healing power. To go to Jerusalem or to Rome was to make a spiritual as well as a physical journey, and pilgrimage was thus a rich metaphor for man's life, a metaphor which was still compelling when Bunyan wrote *Pilgrim's Progress* in the seventeenth century. It is, indeed, one which still has some life today.

The pilgrimage to Canterbury, then, does more than offer a convincing occasion for Chaucer's collection of stories and encounters; it brings into play the possibility of transcendent spiritual truth against which the partial and usually self-interested concerns of the pilgrims may be judged. The extent to which this transcendent truth is actually realised is debatable. Because the image of pilgirmage is so powerful, some writers on the *Canterbury Tales* have argued that the *Parson's Tale* offers an authoritative religious perspective against which the worldly concerns of the other pilgrims are found wanting. However, this view seems not to take into account the formal complexity of the work, to make it too neat and simple. It is not easy, either, to take as authoritative a tale which is, perhaps designedly, a poor example of its genre. It seems more satisfactory to see the Parson's as one, limited, view among others; the product of a character-narrator who, with all his virtues, has no privileged access to truth. On this reading the *Canterbury Tales* leaves unresolved to its end the differences within the society it portrays: the metaphor of pilgrimage serving both to emphasise those differences and their importance.

3 THEMES AND ISSUES IN FRAGMENT 1

3.1 THE *KNIGHT'S TALE* IN ITS CONTEXT

The *Knight's Tale* follows the *General Prologue*, and is in turn followed by the *Miller's Tale*, the *Reeve's Tale* and the unfinished *Cook's Tale*. Together, these works form the first fragment of the *Canterbury Tales* and are bound to one another by various conversations – not to say confrontations – between the pilgrims. Some account of the group, and of the relationships between its parts will suggest fairly well Chaucer's likely plan for the whole work and provide the immediate context in which the *Knight's Tale* occurs.

At the end of the *General Prologue* the pilgrims draw lots to decide who will tell the first story and, in a suspiciously convenient fashion, the lot falls to the Knight, the most important member of the company. The story he tells is a chivalric and courtly romance which seems to glamorise warfare and bravery, and the kind of idealised love I described in 1.4. At its end it is praised as a 'noble storie' by all the company, but particularly by the 'gentils', those pilgrims with some social status.

The Host then calls on the Monk, the next most important member of the company, for his story, and in doing so seems to be making a rather better attempt than the narrator in the *General Prologue* at organising the pilgrims according to their rank. However, the Miller foils him by interrupting drunkenly to say that he has a 'noble tale' with which to 'quite' – to match – the Knight's. His drunkenness wins the day and reluctantly the Host gives him permission to speak, despite objections from the Reeve when he learns that the tale is to be about a carpenter (the Reeve's own trade in his youth).

If there is some disquiet among the pilgrims, the narrator shows even more as he prepares to 'retell' the Miller's story to us, his new audience. He apologises profusely for repeating such a 'cherles tale', but claims he must be a truthful reporter of all that goes on. As a way out of his embarrassment he suggests that those who would prefer not to listen to the Miller or, indeed, to the Reeve who also produces *harlotrie* ought to move on in the book, for there are plenty of stories about 'gentillesse, And eek moralitee and hoolynesse'.

The remarks of the narrator raise again the social question. Words like *cherle*, *vilein*, *gentil*, *gentillesse*, *noble*, are still a part of our vocabulary, but in modern English are used almost exclusively as moral descriptions. In the Middle Ages, however, the words were used just as frequently, and more literally, to define social position. A *vilein* was a man who was unfree, who was still tied to the land and the service of his lord. A *churl* was a man with no social status. *Gentil* and *noble*, by contrast, described someone of aristocratic rank. The narrator, you will notice, treats *gentillesse* as being closely associated with 'moralitee and hoolynesse'. He also assumes that because the Miller is a *cherle* – low class – his story will be morally offensive.

The equation of social *gentillesse* with moral worth was frequent but almost equally frequent in the writing of the time, and particularly so in Chaucer's works, is a questioning of that equation. In the *Canterbury Tales* such questioning occurs in both the *Wife of Bath's Tale* and in the *Franklin's Tale*, and elsewhere in a short poem, 'Gentilesse', Chaucer in his own voice insists that only the virtuous are properly to be called *gentil*.

The narrator's comments then should make us consider carefully how we should judge the Knight's *gentil* tale – is it a seriously moral work or an aristocratic story? We should also consider whether the 'cherles' tales' which follow it are to be dismissed as lightly as the narrator suggests.

3.2 THEMES, SUBJECT MATTER AND PLOTS IN FRAGMENT 1

After this introduction we are already prepared to see the *Miller's Tale* in relation to the *Knight's Tale*, and as we read we are further encouraged to do so by certain similarities between them.

Although the *Knight's Tale* is set in classical Greece and that of the Miller in fourteenth-century Oxford, we have in both a plot in which two young men are in love with the same woman. This time, the woman, Alisoun, is married, and this time the young men are not prepared to worship her from afar, but pursue her vigorously, protesting their love in a rather lower-class version of the language used by Palamon and Arcite. The whole tone of the *Miller's Tale* is different from that of the Knight, for where in the latter love is idealised and seems to have little to do with sex, in the former it is almost entirely a matter of physical enjoyment. Where the *Knight's Tale* presents love, and indeed life, as pain and suffering the *Miller's Tale* seems to revel in the world of the body. Absalon, the unsuccessful lover who has all kinds of pretensions to fashionable behaviour, and is arguably a parody of the Knight's heroes, is mocked and ultimately punished harshly for his posturings and over-refinement.

The *Miller's Tale* ends with a wonderfully farcical conclusion, and afterwards we are returned to the pilgrimage and to the reactions of the pilgrims, particularly to those of the Reeve:

> Diverse folk diversely they seyde,
> But for the moore part they loughe and pleyde.
> Ne at this tale I saugh no man hym greve,
> But it were oonly Osewold the Reve.

The Reeve's anger points, once more, to the social conflict important to the whole work, for reeves and millers were proverbially enemies. A reeve managed his lord's estate and was in charge of running it as profitably as possible, and the local miller if he were dishonest was likely to reduce those profits when the lord's corn was ground.

Oswald's reactions link with darker themes, though, for his anger expresses itself in an outburst against his own sexual impotence, the horrors of old age and of approaching death. For him as for Theseus, death is the dominating fact of life:

> For sikerly, whan I was bore, anon
> Deeth drough the tappe of lyf and leet it gon;
> And ever sithe hath so the tappe yronne
> Til that almoost al empty is the tonne.
> The streem of lyf now droppeth on the chymbe.

Here we are taken back to the *Knight's Tale*, where death is the only certainty, and pain and loss lie beneath the bright pageantry which men try to create.

The *Reeve's Tale* itself, however, makes very different sense of the human condition and of human love from either of its predecessors, for it has none of the idealism of the one nor the delight of the other. Instead, it rather sourly reduces sex to just one more counter in the point-scoring game which is life.

The *Cook's Tale*, the last in Fragment 1, is unfinished, but looks as though it were intended to be another 'cherle's tale', so it may be that

Chaucer was intent on showing us the variety of ways of looking at the world which that contemptuous term could embrace. However, we have no way of knowing absolutely because he wrote only about seventy lines of it.

Fragment 1, then, is bound together in a variety of ways; by connections and contrasts in themes, subject matter and plot so that we are constantly encouraged to place the Knight's assumptions about the world against those of his fellow pilgrims.

3.3   THE DIFFERENT GENRES OF FRAGMENT 1

In the *General Prologue* Chaucer makes use of the genre of estates satire. In the rest of Fragment 1 he uses two other genres, that of the romance in the *Knight's Tale*, and the fabliau in the Miller's and Reeve's tales.

That Chaucer chooses to use such different genres seems of some importance, for different genres, different kinds of story, embody different attitudes to life and make different assumptions about it. Thus the genre of a literary work is a part of its meaning. In the case of a deeply ironic poet such as Chaucer the implicit assumptions of any particular genre may be brought to the surface by tensions within a work, or by contrasts between works of different genres. We are thus enabled to question these assumptions instead of accepting them unconsciously.

Estates satire works on the assumption that the different groups of which society is composed are necessary to one another, and could work together harmoniously if all their members worked together properly. A metaphor often used, even today, and one which you may well recognise from reading Shakespeare is that of the 'body politic'. Just as every limb is necessary to the proper functioning of the body so every member (and 'member' is an old world for limb) in a society has his or her proper part to play. Each contributes to the 'common weal', (our word 'Commonwealth') the good of all. But, as I have argued in 2.2, Chaucer's use of estates satire seems to work towards undermining this assumption of the genre by making us feel that such mutual supportiveness is not really a possibility in the society he portrays.

The sense of a society made up of groups with conflicting values is enforced as Fragment 1 continues by the way in which the Knight's romance and the Miller's and Reeve's fabliaux are not merely placed side by side, but in competition with one another.

What assumptions about human life, then, do we find in romance? First of all, the world of romance is exclusive. It is assumed that ideally, and for most practical purposes, high birth and moral virtue are inseparable. Some romances, mainly early ones, place an emphasis on war and fighting, and are concerned with heroic exploits. Their heroes are honourable, brave, strong, skilful, fierce in battle, and yet gentle to the weak. In rather later romance the emphasis shifts a little, and while there is nearly always an interest in marvellous doings and adventures, love becomes central to the story, the kind of love I described in 1.4. Romance has a vocabulary of moral terms which you will recognise from the description of the Knight and the Squire in the *General Prologue*. *Trouthe* is all important, and in the context of romance nearly always has the sense of 'loyalty', 'promise-keeping'. To break one's *trouthe*, whatever the circumstances, is an unpardonable sin. *Curteisie* is also central, and often means rather more than courtly, good-mannered behaviour. It can suggest an inner disposition from which such behaviour springs. In a number of romances an apparently low-born hero astonishes other characters by the fineness and delicacy of his behaviour, given the disadvantages of his upbringing. Needless to say, despite appearances to the contrary, he is, almost without exception, of noble birth.

Honour is another important value and is the respect in which one is held, or – equally important – the respect which one shows to others. It is also – and here it connects with *trouthe* – the behaviour which earns respect. *Largesse*, *fredom*, *franchise* are closely related, and usually have the sense of 'generosity'. The last two words also have at times associations similar to our 'freedom'. To call someone 'free', then, can suggest that he is spontaneous, carelessly generous, without regard to, or fear of, consequences – a privilege afforded to few in a society in which most scratched for a living and owed service to their lords.

Both the content and vocabulary of romance express aristocratic values, and underwrite a hierarchical society in which virtue and admirable behaviour are seen almost exclusively as the preserve of those with power, and in doing so they give their support to and glamorise the prevailing social structure.

The fabliau presents us with a very different world. Although fabliaux were enjoyed by aristocratic audiences their characters tend to be bourgeois, townspeople, merchants and not very well-behaved priests and friars and monks. The stories tend to be about sexual and/or financial trickery. They are usually comic; bawdy and cynical;

we are invited to laugh at and admire the tricksters rather than to disapprove of them. Fabliaux assume that people are out for their own ends, and that life is a competitive business. In them figures of authority – more often than not rich husbands – are mocked, together with the values of romance. Love is reduced to sex, deceit takes the place of *trouthe*, and to win is all-important.

In the first fragment of the *Canterbury Tales,* then, Chaucer uses side by side genres which present different, indeed, opposed values. Moreover, the linking passages in which the Miller claims that he will 'quite' the Knight, and in which the narrator worries over his 'cherles tale' encourage us to see the tales as rival versions of reality, and to regard these different versions of reality as being connected with the social positions of their tellers.

4 THE *KNIGHT'S TALE*: SUMMARY AND CRITICAL COMMENTARY

SUMMARY

The plot of the *Knight's Tale* concerns the love of Palamon and Arcite, two young Thebans, for Emily, the sister-in-law of their victorious enemy, Theseus, ruler of Athens. The young men fall in love with Emily when they catch sight of her from the window of the prison to which Theseus has consigned them for life after the destruction of Thebes. Their love for her dominates the action of the rest of the tale.

Arcite is eventually released from prison through the pleas of Perotheus, Theseus's life-long friend, and after some years of illness caused by his love returns in disguise to Athens where he lives as a servant in Theseus's court. Palamon escapes from prison, and as he is hiding in a wood outside Athens, encounters Arcite. They fight over Emily, and are discovered by Theseus and his court. Theseus pardons them and arranges for a great tournament to be held the following year to decide which of them should marry Emily.

Both lovers return with their followers at the appointed time, and after Palamon, Arcite and Emily have prayed to their respective gods, Venus, Mars and Diana, the tournament is fought. Arcite is victorious, but is killed in his moment of triumph through the machinations of the god Saturn. He is buried with great honour, and after a lapse of time Theseus gives Emily in marriage to Palamon.

The tale is divided into four parts, perhaps marking suitable breaks if the work were to be read aloud over a number of evenings.

For the modern reader probably the most striking characteristic of the *Knight's Tale* is its formality, its grave and ceremonious movement. Many aspects of the work contribute towards this formality. There is, first of all, the way in which it is told. A leisurely effect is created by a concentration upon important scenes and speeches while intervening events, often taking place over a long stretch of time, are swiftly summarised. We are given a series of set scenes, often ornate and full of detail, which are frequently arranged so that their events fall into a pattern. There is patterning, too, between scenes as well as within them so that one scene parallels or contrasts with another. Thus, the very way in which the story is told encourages us to find order and meaning in its events.

Treatment of character also accentuates the formality and pattern of the work, for the characters, although we may be moved by their fates, do not emerge as individuals but exist solely to fulfil their function in the plot. Emily is the idealised courtly heroine, little more than the love-object of Palamon and Arcite, and almost without a voice. Arcite and Palamon themselves stay firmly within their roles as lovers, arguably as like as two peas in a pod (although some critics have claimed that the characters are rather different). Theseus acts entirely as conqueror and ruler, and we never see him in any private capacity.

Theseus, however, occupies a rather different place in the story from the other human characters. Where the rest are passive, very much the playthings of chance and the gods, Theseus is active. It is he who tries to shape events and to impose order on human actions and emotions; on the accidents of fortune. It is he, finally, who asserts the existence of a divine order. In his manipulation of characters and events one might see him as being rather like the author himself. Just as the author arranges the events of the story so that we see them as parts of a pattern, so Theseus, his character *within* the story, tries to act on, to order his world. We thus have a formally ordered work whose story is itself about the imposition of order, so that style and content interact with one another very interestingly. Characters behave with great ceremony, and this belongs both to the way in which the story is written, and to the society which Theseus rules. Theseus, the hero of Greek myth, has been given the manners and values of a fourteenth-century ruler, his formality and concern with rank and hierarchy reminiscent of the ceremony of Richard II's Court.

I have said that Theseus is the great shaper; finally the expounder of a divine, hierarchical order. Into this order, he claims, all the apparently accidental and painful events of men's lives – including death, the one event common to all – can be seen to fit. Because the tale itself is so formally ordered, you may decide that Chaucer is giving a special authority to Theseus, that he is the real hero of the tale, and it is his perspective the reader is intended to accept. If so, then you might read the tale as a celebration and endorsement of medieval aristocratic values and life-style; or perhaps of the way in which ceremony and order give sense and meaning to human life.

It is important to notice, however, that the very formality of the tale underlines the disorder and cruelty of the events it describes, and that Theseus's actions are not unequivocally effective, or even praiseworthy. We might also think that it is not too easy to see the world we have had created for us in terms of the divine order which Theseus asserts. If this is the case, then it is possible to read the tale as a criticism rather than a celebration of the values of the social group the Knight, its narrator, represents. On this reading, Theseus is likely to be the Knight's hero, but not necessarily Chaucer's.

Because Chaucer hides behind a series of narrators in the *Canterbury Tales* (see 2.3 and 3.1) we, as readers, are often forced into unusual activity in judging and interpreting, and are likely to find that our own values play a significant part in our interpretations. However, once we accept that there are no easy answers to what Chaucer 'really' thought we discover that part of the pleasure of reading the *Canterbury Tales* lies in the discussion it provokes, and, perhaps, in its capacity to reveal to us our own hidden values and assumptions.

Part I of The *Knight's Tale* (Robinson, I 859–1354)

In this section of the poem Theseus rides home to Athens with his bride Hippolyta, queen of the Amazons whom he has conquered. With them is Hippolyta's young sister Emily. Outside Athens they are met by a group of mourning women who ask Theseus's help. Creon, conqueror of Thebes, has refused burial to the bodies of their defeated husbands. Theseus conquers Thebes and restores the bones of their husbands to the women. Palamon and Arcite are discovered among the dead and wounded outside the city and taken to Athens where Theseus consigns them to perpetual imprisonment. While in prison they see Emily from their window, fall in love with her, quarrel, and complain about their fates.

The tale opens with a conventional formula, the equivalent of 'once upon a time . . . , – Whilom, as olde stories tellen us . . . (859). Theseus, the 'lord and governour' of Athens is introduced, and the events leading up to the beginning of the story summarised, even as its teller by means of the rhetorical device of *occupatio* declares his intention of *not* doing so:

> I wolde have toold yow fully the manere
> How wonnen was the regne of Femenye . . .
> . . .
> But al that thyng I moot as now forbere.   (876–885)

We are then reminded that the tale is the Knight's contribution to the story-telling contest:

> Lat every felawe telle his tale aboute,
> And lat se now who shal the soper wynne;   (890–1)

After this introduction the tale focuses on Theseus riding to Athens 'In al his wele and in his mooste pride' and on his encounter with the mourning women who ask him to redress the 'vileynye', the wrong, that Creon has done to their husbands in denying their bodies burial. The encounter is described in some detail, but it is worth noticing how selective this detail is; the stress is all on the behaviour of the women, the speech of their leader, and on the reactions of Theseus. There is no attempt to create a concrete physical context for the meeting.

Despite the grief of the women the encounter is ceremonious. The women, clothed in black, are arranged two by two. The eldest, their spokeswoman, greets Theseus formally:

> Lord, to whom Fortune hath yiven
> Victorie   (915–16)

In keeping with this formality, her appeal to Theseus is that he should restore a broken social and human order, for the grief of the women is not so much at the death of their husbands as at the contempt, the denial of their status, which Creon has shown to the bodies. The plight of the women is assumed to be the more painful because of their high rank:

> For, certes, lord, ther is noon of us alle,
> That she ne hath been a duchesse or a queene.   (922–3)

Just as high rank and sensitivity to suffering are associated, so Theseus's *gentillesse* is assumed by the ladies to entail sensitivity to the sufferings of others:

> Som drope of pitee, thurgh thy gentillesse,
> Upon us wrecched wommen lat thou falle.   (920–1)

Theseus's response to their pleas does not disappoint their expectations, and contrasts sharply with Creon's *vileynye*

> This gentil duc doun from his courser sterte
> With herte pitous . . .   (952–3)

Like the ladies themselves, he sees their former 'greet estaat' as making their present situation the more pitiable, and as 'trewe knyght' vows vengeance on Creon.

Throughout the episode both characters and narrator seem to assume that the proper social order is hierarchical and that *gentillesse* of rank must be duly maintained; not only must the bodies of the noble be buried with proper ceremony, both Theseus and the women must treat one another with the respect their status requires. Moreover, the *gentillesse* of Theseus is comprehensive, there is no attempt in the passage to distinguish between his high birth and his moral worth. Social and moral *gentillesse* are regarded as indistinguishable here, with *gentillesse* of rank entailing a superior sensitivity to the sufferings of others.

Theseus, who in his swift and sympathetic response to the ladies is presented as a text-book ruler, is further glamorised in the short description of his riding to battle:

> The rede statue of Mars, with spere and targe,
> So shyneth in his white baner large,
> That alle the feeldes glyteren up and doun;
> And by his baner born is his penoun
> Of gold ful riche, in which ther was ybete
> The Mynotaur, which that he slough in Crete.
> Thus rit this duc, thus rit this conquerour,
> And in his hoost of chivalrie the flour,   (975–82)

The scene is described from a distance, and the flashes of colour, of red and white and gold, the fields glittering with the banners of Theusus's army evoke its visual splendour. The Minotaur (the monster that the Theseus of Greek myth killed in the labyrinth) on his pennant serves to remind us of his past exploits. The repetition of 'Thus rit this duc, thus rit . . . ' and the traditional description of Theseus as 'of chivalrie the flour' help to present the exploit as magnificent, to suppress for the moment any awareness that war is destructive.

The siege of Thebes is dealt with quickly, almost perfunctorily, Creon slain in fair fight, and the bones of the husbands restored to their ladies. Yet within these few lines we are made aware that the destruction of Thebes is complete and devastating. The city is won 'And Rente adoun bothe walle and sparre and rafter;' We are made aware, too, of the disorder and pain which follow battle, of the piles of bodies among whom the pillagers root. When Palamon and Arcite are discovered they are 'torn' from the heaps of dead and dying, and the lots of victor and vanquished are sharply contrasted:

> And ther he lyveth in joye and in honour
> Terme of his lyf; what nedeth wordes mo?
> And in a tour, in angwissh and in wo,
> This Palamon and his felawe Arcite
> For everemoore . . .   (1028–32)

Stressed, too, (it is mentioned twice) is Theseus's refusal to allow Palamon and Arcite to be ransomed, the common medieval practice for noble prisoners.

The tale then registers, almost as an aside, a considerable lapse of time 'This passeth yeer by yeer and day by day' (1003) before we are taken into one of the most important episodes of the tale; Palamon's and Arcite's first sight of Emily.

The lengthy episode begins with a leisurely description of Emily, walking early on a May morning in the garden next to Palamon's and Arcite's prison, singing and gathering flowers. The season, her golden-haired beauty and her conventionally courtly pursuits all define her as a heroine of romance, and yet the description of her transcends that convention. Her beauty is not so much described as evoked, conveyed by her comparison with 'the lylie upon his stalke grene', by her association with the 'floures newe' of May. Even her colouring is flower-like 'For with the rose colour stroof hire hewe' (1038). The image created is not so much that of a beautiful woman as of the spring itself, with all its freshness and life. As she walks in the garden we are given the one specific detail of her hair; its colour, length and style noted, and then she dissolves again into something almost insubstantial 'And as an aungel hevenysshly she soong' (1055). Set against the freedom of this delicate image with all its flower-like fragility is 'The grete tour, that was so thikke and stroong' (1056) in which Palamon moves about restlessly. The contrast between Emily's freedom and his restriction is brought out by the repetition of the word *romed*. Palamon roams in 'a chambre an heigh', and a few lines later:

> this fresshe Emelye the shene
> Was in hire walk, and romed up and doun.
> This sorweful prisoner, this Palamoun,
> Goth in the chambre romyng to and fro,
> And to hymself compleynynge of his wo.   (1068–72)

The harshness of the prison is emphasised by the description of the window through which Palamon sees Emily

> a wyndow, thikke of many a barre
> Of iren greet and square as any sparre.   (1075–6)

The sight of Emily causes Palamon to cry out 'As though he stongen were unto the herte' (1079). Arcite, misinterpreting the cause of his emotion, advises him to take his imprisonment with patience, to accept the inevitable, and blames their predicament on Fortune. In this he is like the women of the earlier episode, though *he* defines Fortune as the influence of the planets rather than the blind goddess turning her wheel.

Like Palamon, however, Arcite is overwhelmed by the sight of Emily, and the two quarrel, their vows of loyalty to one another quickly dissolved in their new rivalry.

Once more, the passage is formal and stylised, and both Palamon and Arcite use the conventional metaphors of courtly love to express their feelings. Love is a wound to the heart, a wound received through the eye, the beauty of Emily has power to kill; for her to return the love of one of them would be a gift; her mercy, her grace. The similarity of the lovers' reactions is stressed by the similarity of the vocabulary used to describe them:

> He cast his eye upon Emelya,
> And therwithal he bleynte and cride, 'A!'
> As though he stongen were unto the herte.
>   (Palamon)   (1077–9)

> And with that sighte hir beautee hurte hym so,
> That, if that Palamon was wounded sore,
> Arcite is hurt as muche as he, or moore.
>   (Arcite)   (1114–6)

> I was hurt right now thurghout myn ye
> Into myn herte, that wol my bane be.
>   (Palamon)   (1096–7)

> The fresshe beautee sleeth me sodeynly
> Of hire that rometh in the yonder place
>
> (Arcite)   (1118-9)

Despite their conventionality, these metaphors seem poignant and moving, given weight by the lovers' imprisonment and, eventually, by the death of Arcite. Palamon's prayer to Emily when he imagines her to be Venus further underlines their suffering.

The episode in which Palamon and Arcite quarrel is stylised not only in the conventionality of the language it uses to describe love but also in the symmetrical arrangement of the lovers' long speeches, which are more like operatic arias than the stuff of conversation. There is only the odd physical detail 'This Palamon gan knytte his browes tweye' – to remind us that Palamon and Arcite are more than voices.

The very formality of their speeches emphasises, however, the way in which the lovers' feelings work to destroy promises and obligations, all the rules that create social order. Each accuses the other of promise-breaking, of breaking too, the ties of their blood relationship; they are kinsmen and have sworn an oath of loyalty to one another, pledged themselves to *forthren* each other *trewely* in their loves on pain of death. It belongs to them as knights to keep their *trouthe*. Palamon first insists on this:

> I loved hire first, and tolde thee my wo
> As to my conseil and my brother sworn
> To forthre me . . .   (1146-8)

Arcite begins by returning Palamon's accusation of falseness:

> thou art fals, I telle thee outrely,
> For paramour I loved hire first er thow,   (1154-5)

He justifies his claim by a legalistic hair-splitting over the definition of love; his love is love for a woman, Palamon's, since he has mistaken Emily for Venus, is 'affeccioun of hoolynesse', a quite different emotion. Again, his language echoes that of Palamon:

> For which I tolde thee myn aventure
> As to my cosyn and my brother sworn.   (1160-1)

Arcite's arguments do not rest here however; his next assertion contradicts not only Palamon's claims for the importance of promise-keeping but his own as well as he argues that the power of love is strong enough to dissolve all promises and rules. 'Love is a gretter lawe', he insists. The tone of the speech then changes, and becomes distanced and cynical as he reminds Palamon of the unreality of their quarrel:

> For wel thou woost thyselven, verraily,
> That thou and I be dampned to prisoun
> Perpetuelly; us gayneth no raunsoun. (1174–6)

The heavy beat of the lines, the stress placed on *perpetuelly* by enjambment (the sentence carries on without pause over the line ending), the repetitive 'us gayneth no raunsoun' brings a dark note into the dispute.

Arcite's next words, his homely simile comparing the lovers to two dogs fighting over a bone, are a sudden disquieting switch from the earlier, elevated language of love, underlining the ludicrousness of the quarrel. They also make us aware of the possessiveness lying beneath the apparent humility and submission of the lovers' fine speeches. Finally Emily is no more than an object to be fought over.

The quarrel is followed by a very compressed account of Arcite's reprieve at the request of Perotheus, Theseus's life-long friend. Despite the brevity of the account we are reminded, by means of the device of *occupatio*, of another story, this time of loyalty between friends:

> So wel they lovede, as olde bookes sayn,
> That whan that oon was deed, soothly to telle,
> His felawe wente and soughte hym doun in helle, –
> But of that storie list me nat to write. (1198–1201)

The terms of Arcite's release are defined legalistically and the passage ends on a note of threat, emphasising the consequences if Arcite should be tempted to return to Athens 'Lat hym be war! his nekke lith to wedde' (1218). Then the pace of the narrative slows down once more, and once more we have two symmetrical, formal complaints from the lovers in which, despite their physical situation, they seem to vie with one another in bewailing the unpredictability of life and the harshness of their respective fates. Both describe a world which is beyond man's control.

Arcite's complaint is preceded by the narrator's hyperbolic account of his sufferings in which apostrophe and repetition combine to insist upon their intensity:

> How greet a sorwe suffreth now Arcite!
> The deeth he feeleth thurgh his herte smyte;
> He wepeth, wayleth, crieth pitously;   (1219–21)

Arcite's own language is predictably extreme; to be deprived of the sight of Emily is 'helle', 'prisoun' near her is 'paradys', his misery is 'eternal'. He apostrophises the absent Palamon, 'O deere cosyn Palamon' whom he describes as being in 'blisse'. In contrast with the everlasting hell he sees for himself he imagines Palamon as favoured by 'chaungeable' Fortune 'Wel hath Fortune yturned thee the dys' (1238) and able because of his nearness to Emily to advance his position with her. The speech is operatic, full of exclamations; the despair it expresses complete and not to be alleviated. Emily, the woman to whom he has never spoken, becomes the whole of his life 'Farewel my lif, my lust, and my gladnesse!' (1250). From the contemplation of his present misery he moves into regret that his prayers have been answered; in this unpredictable world it is dangerous to pray, better to accept the 'purveiaunce of God, or of Fortune', for we can never know what disasters our prayers, answered, will bring. Repetition – 'Som man desireth . . .som man wolde' adds weight to his claim that 'Infinite harmes been in this mateere' (1259). After this rhetorical outburst the everyday image of men going through the world as drunk as a mouse makes us feel his helplessness in a world where the gods move so mysteriously.

Palamon's misery is described in even more exaggerated terms than that of Arcite. The hyperbole (overstatement) is so strong that it introduces a comic note, distancing us from its subject; the word *youlyng*, for example, seems contemptuous. 'Weeping' might be a suitable reaction, but *youlyng* sounds child-like and undignified. The literalness, too, of the detail of Arcite's fetters being wet with tears seems absurd.

The lines in which Palamon imagines Arcite returning with an army to win Emily by force recalls Arcite's image of the dogs and bone, for once more Emily is seen as an object to be acquired and not as a person with wishes of her own.

Interestingly, each character sees his own fate as fixed, and that of the other as open to improvement, but where Arcite's speech has emphasised the unpredictability of men's lives, Palamon stresses their powerlessness. His misery expresses itself in a series of questions which contain their own answers:

> What is mankynde moore unto you holde
> Than is the sheep that rouketh in the folde?

> For slayn is man right as another beest
>
> . . .
>
> What governance is in this prescience,
> That giltelees tormenteth innocence?   (1307–14)

Men's lives are foredoomed, their events already written by the gods; there is no room for alteration and prayer will do no good. The gods, moreover, are cruel and uncaring, men no more to them than the beasts. Innocence and guilt are irrelevant. These questions emphasise Palamon's sense of injustice and pain, and as his despair grows he sees men's conditions as worse than that of the animals, for men are forced to deny their desires at the bidding of the gods and condemned to pain after death.

Palamon then blames his own fate on the hatred of the goddess Juno for the people of Thebes (In Greek myth this was because of Jupiter's infidelity with Semele, daughter of Cadmus, the founder of the city).

The speeches of the lovers, stressing the helplessness of men, form a climax to the first part of the poem. Fortune, introduced in the episode of the women, her wrongs seemingly redressed by Theseus there, has become all-important and is now associated with the gods. We may see Theseus as the instrument of Fortune in the lives of the lovers, introducing misery and chaos rather than restoring order. At the same time, we have been made to realise that threats to the social order come not only through the workings of external chance, but through human emotions, for Palamon and Arcite quarrel and break their vows to one another because of their love for Emily.

There is thus a shift of perspective within this first part, for at the beginning we have been asked to see events from Theseus's standpoint, to applaud the way in which he has upheld a proper social hierarchy, but when we move to the predicament of Palamon and Arcite we see that his actions have affected some lives in a precisely opposite way.

As well as this broad shift in perspective there are small, localised shifts, caused by changes in tone; the images of the dogs and the bone, of man as drunk as a mouse, Palamon's slightly comic grief, the narrator's casual glossing over of years of imprisonment.

These shifts raise in the reader the same questions that Palamon and Arcite ask. What kind of sense can human life make when it is shown to be so vulnerable? What does love or friendship amount to in the poem?

Typically, at the end of the first section the narrator distances us from his characters, showing them to be completely under his control

'Now wol I stynte of Palamon a lite' (1334). This distance is increased as, charcteristically again, he addresses his audience, asking which of the lovers has the worst of things. The fact that this question may seem to us irrelevant or fairly trivial only has the effect of making us ask our own questions harder.

Part II of the *Knight's Tale* (Robinson, I 1355–1880)

The second part of the *Knight's Tale* is as formally structured as the first. The fortunes of Palamon and Arcite are dealt with in turn. Arcite, after a long illness, returns in disguise to Athens, and Palamon escapes from prison. We have their encounter in the grove outside Athens, Theseus's discovery of them fighting, and his plan for a great tournament to decide which of the two will marry Emily. The section ends, in sharp contrast with Part One, with Palamon and Arcite riding away joyfully to recruit their company of knights for the tournament.

At the beginning of Part Two Arcite's sufferings are described in clinical detail; his symptoms are quite literally those of love-sickness, a physical disease, as it is described in medieval books of medicine. For almost the first time in the tale we have something like extended physical description:

> lene he wex and drye as is a shaft;
> His eyen holwe, and grisly to biholde,
> His hewe falow and pale as asshen colde,   (1362–4)

The scientific precision with which Arcite's state is described leaves us in no doubt about the reality of his illness; it is like mania as well as love-sickness, we are told, and mania is defined for us in physiological terms: the brain is divided into three cells, the first controlling the imagination, the second reason and the third memory. It is in the front cell controlling the imagination that Arcite's illness seems to be located. At the same time, while the tone of the whole description is clinical, the comparisons 'drye as is a shaft', 'pale as asshen colde' suggest a spiritual as well as a physical state.

Having established the seriousness of Arcite's condition the narrator cuts himself short, sliding quite casually over the length of his sufferings:

> What sholde I al day of his wo endite?
> Whan he endured hadde a yeer or two
> This crueel torment and this peyne and wo,   (1380–2)

Notice how the perfunctory 'a yeere or two' jars against 'crueel torment', 'peyne and wo' here, and so serves to distance us a little.

The narrator then describes Arcite's dream of Mercury, the messenger of the gods. Interestingly, he refers here to the story of Argus, the hundred-eyed watchman whom Mercury lulls to sleep with his shaft. Perhaps the 'slepy yerde' Mercury carries in his dream is to be taken as a sign that he will guard Arcite from Theseus's vigilance; certainly the reference is a reminder that we are in the realm of Greek myth.

The dream visitation arouses Arcite to life and resolution 'And with that word Arcite wook and sterte'. His resulting perceptions, actions and intentions are listed in a series of lines mostly beginning with 'And . . . '. This patterning suggests both the purposefulness of his behaviour, and also the way in which it is dominated by his hopes for the future.

Although Arcite's life in Theseus's court is described in some detail, the effect is that of a summary, an explanation of his success. Notice, though, that Arcite cannot be left as a humble servant; his *gentillesse* is not to be disguised (see 3.2):

> He was so gentil of condicioun
> That thurghout al the court was his renoun   (1431–32)

This episode ends with the kind of narrative joke to which we have become accustomed 'And in this blisse lete I now Arcite' (1449). The narrator's suggestion that Arcite has an existence outside the confines of the poem serves in fact to emphasise his status as a fictional character.

The narrator then dwells upon Palamon's miserable plight. As in his treatment of Arcite, however, there is a movement from apparent involvement to a kind of facetious detachment:

> Who koude ryme in Englyssh proprely
> His martirdom? for sothe it am nat I;
> Therfore I passe as lightly as I may.   (1459–61)

The ostensible message may be that Palamon's suffering is too extreme to be described, but the idea of rhyming it in English enforces, just as the narrator's unceremonious shifts of subject have done, that after all, Palamon is just a character in a story, a story, moreover, in which seven years can be dealt with in four lines.

The description of Palamon's escape from prison parallels in its perfunctoriness that of Arcite's residence at Theseus's court. The sole, rather niggling detail of the kind of drug Palamon uses on his gaoler is its only gesture towards credibility. Notice, though, that in the midst of this brief description the narrator can find time to echo Arcite's and Palamon's earlier questioning of destiny:

> Were it by aventure or destynee –
> As, whan a thyng is shapen, it shal be –   (1465–6)

The summary of Palamon's intentions on his escape recalls Arcite's state of mind as he moves back to Athens, so that we are given a sense of the two characters moving irresistibly towards one another; an effect heightened by the narrator's 'Now wol I turne to Arcite ageyn' (1488).

The episode in which Palamon and Arcite meet opens with a rhetorical flourish as the break of day is described in a series of personifications. The lark, Phoebus the sun, the east itself, are all humanised; the lark is *bisy*, the 'messager of day', it *salueth* the morning; the east *laugheth*. The image created of the morning is full of brightness; 'firy Phebus', 'silver dropes'. This is high style, designed to give importance to the writer's subject, and Arcite is similarly glamorised as he rides on 'a courser, startlynge as the fir' to gather greenery to celebrate May, the traditional season of lovers.

Arcite rides, and the coincidence is stressed, to the very wood where Palamon hides, and the narrator takes the opportunity to sermonise on the way in which the unexpected intervenes in human affairs. He maintains this distance from his characters, continuing to use them as examples of common behaviour, as he comments on Arcite's changeability of mood. Arcite is presented to us, not as an individual, but as a typical lover with his 'queynte geres'. The proverbial tone of the whole passage helps to establish his typicality, as the narrator concludes 'Selde is the Friday al the wowke ylike' (1539). The narrator's detachment disappears, however, as Arcite moves into the kind of lament so typical of these lovers; one which takes us back to Palamon's in Part One, and once more Juno's hatred of Thebes is referred to. Previously Arcite has lamented the uncertainty of life, and the inscrutability of the gods; now, like Palamon, he attributes his misfortunes to their anger. His sense of doom is expressed rhetorically as he apostrophises Juno:

> 'Allas,' quod he, 'that day that I was bore!
> How longe, Juno, thurgh thy crueltee,
> Woltow werreyen Thebes the citee?   (1342–4)

When he describes his love, his images are, as usual, both conventional and extreme:

> Love hath his firy dart so brennyngly
> Ystiked thurgh my trewe, careful herte,
> That shapen was my deeth erst than my sherte. (1564–6)

Palamon, overhearing this speech, breaks into a counterpart, but first his anger is described, entirely by a concentration on his physical appearance and sensations. It is a 'coold swerd' through his heart, he shakes with anger, his face is 'deed and pale', and he behaves as though he were mad. Once more he accuses Arcite of treachery and promise-breaking, not only to himself now, but to Theseus as well. The quarrel with Arcite must be settled by fighting, and he is prepared to die or to kill. Notice that he is jealous of anyone other than himself loving Emily; not of Emily preferring someone to himself.

Arcite, 'fiers as leon', in language somewhat less than formal, restates his earlier position:

> What, verray fool, thynk wel that love is free,
> And I wol love hire maugree al thy myght! (1606–7)

Arcite, however, tries to bring their conflict under the rules of knightly behaviour, and insists on bringing the proper equipment for them both:

> Have heer my trouthe . . .
> That heere I wol be founden as a knyght,
> And bryngen harneys right ynough for the;
> And ches the beste, and leef the worste for me.
> (1610–14)

The fight is thus delayed, and the narrator, apostrophising Cupid, comments rather platitudinously on the divisiveness of love:

> O Cupide, out of alle charitee!
> A regne, that wolt no felawe have with thee!
> (1623–4)

Arcite's collection of the armour is summarised briefly, with the one specific detail of his carrying the gear in front of him on his saddle giving weight to his preparations.

   The reactions of the lovers when they meet one another before
battle are conveyed by means of the extended simile likening them
to hunters of Thrace when faced with their prey. The use of extended
simile is part of medieval high style which confers dignity and
importance on its subject. Thus, Palamon's and Arcite's encounter is
given something of an heroic status at this point. However, the
content of the simile in which hunters are faced with 'the leon or the
bere . . . russhyng in the greves' prepares the way for the lovers'
lapse into animal behaviour only a few lines later. They may begin by
helping each other to arm, each 'as freendly as he were his owene
brother', but soon descend to savagery. They are described as mad
animals, as lions, tigers, boars. Their savagery is emphasised by
comparison embedded within comparison, and also by hyperbole,
which, as on earlier occasions, distances us from them:

> As *wilde bores* gonne they to smyte,
> That frothen *whit as foom* for ire wood.
> Up to the ancle foghte they in hir blood.
>
> (1658–60)

   Immediately after these lines, however, there is an abrupt change
of tone as the narrator tells us in one of his customary little jokes that
he will leave them fighting while he turns to Theseus:

> And in this wise I lete hem fightyng dwelle,
> And forth I wole of Theseus yow telle.   (1661–2)

   He then asserts the power of destiny in men's lives, and the
existence of a divine plan. This passage has the effect of foreground-
ing the coincidences which have come thick and fast, and thus
reminds us that the story is a fiction. It takes us back again, too, to
question the kind of order governing men's lives. Notice that the
narrator, unlike his characters who believe in the gods or fortune,
speaks of 'The purveiaunce that God hath seyn biforn' (1665) not
only suggesting himself as a Christian writing about pagans, but
producing yet another explanation of man's destiny.
   Theseus's hunting is described as service to Diana, the goddess of
hunting. There is a word-play here, however, for Diana is also the
goddess of chastity whom Hippolyta had served before her marriage.
We are then given a more than usually detailed account of the
reasons for Theseus's hunting in the very grove where Arcite and
Palamon are fighting. Possibly this detail invites us to think about

how an explanation of events in terms of destiny or providence fits with more everyday explanations:

> And to the grove that stood ful faste by,
> In which ther was an hert, as men hym tolde,
> Duc Theseus the streighte wey hath holde.
>
> (1688–90)

Theseus's intervention in the lovers' fight is swift and forceful:

> And at a stert he was bitwix hem two,
> And pulled out a swerd, and cride 'Hoo!'
>
> (1705–6)

Notice that he reacts first of all to the lawlessness of the fight, the absence of 'juge or oother officere'. Palamon's reply to Theseus displays the way in which his love has completely destroyed all his vows of loyalty, for he betrays Arcite immediately. He is happy to die so long as Arcite does too.

Like the lovers, Theseus can be overwhelmed by anger. On hearing who they are, 'he first for ire quook and sterte', but the narrator is concerned to show that truly *gentil* behaviour can control anger, and there is a kind of exchange of *gentillesse* running through the passage; the women weep because the lovers are *gentil* and beg Theseus to spare them; he does so because *he* is *gentil* 'For pitee renneth soone in gentil herte' (1761) but of course the women are *gentil* too, and it is their *pitee* which moves Theseus. Notice that *gentillesse* and *pitee* have already been strongly associated in the episode of the mourning women at the beginning of the poem.

The women's prayers move Theseus, even more importantly, to the exercise of his reason, and he explicitly restrains himself from the kind of mad, animal behaviour of Palamon and Arcite. Discretion, reason, measure, become his values. His speech, after the extremities of the lovers, the weeping of the women and his own anger strikes a dismissive note. True, it starts in the high style to which we have become accustomed:

> 'The god of love, a, *benedicite*!
> How myghty and how greet a lord is he!'
>
> (1785–6)

However, the tone soon establishes itself as ironic:

> Now looketh, is nat that an heigh folye?
> Who may been a fool, but if he love? (1798–9)

The contemptuous amusement deepens as Theseus drops from his ironic high style to describe the love of Palamon and Arcite in very unelevated terms:

> But this is yet the beste game of alle,
> That she for whom they han this jolitee
> Kan hem therfore as muche thank as me.
> She woot namoore of al this hoote fare,
> By God, than woot a cokkow or an hare!
>
> (1806–10)

Through the comparison of Emily with a cuckoo or a hare their love, a matter of life, death and high sentiments to them, is defined as no more than a physical urge; and made the more ridiculous because of Emily's unconsciousness of their existence. Theseus, however, accuses himself of the same folly – he too has been love's servant in his youth – and ritualises their rivalry by his plan for the tournament to be held the following year.

Once more, it is important to notice, Theseus is acting as a shaper, the imposer of a proper order on himself and on the world around him. He has controlled his own anger, and rescues Palamon and Arcite from their descent into animal ferocity, imposing rules upon their enmity, making of it something to be settled with proper ceremony.

Part III (Robinson, I 1881–2482)

In some ways this is the crucial section of the tale; it is certainly the most ornate, and yet within it the action is advanced hardly at all. It opens with an extended description of the lists, including the temples of the gods set in their walls. There is an account of the return of Palamon and Arcite to Athens with their companies of knights, each led by an exotic champion who is described in detail; a description of Palamon, Emily and Arcite praying to their respective gods, and finally the quarrel between Mars and Venus, with Saturn promising his intervention. Both gods have promised that the prayers of their servants will be answered, and we are left to await Saturn's solution.

The magnificent lists, built in the place where Arcite and Palamon first fought, on one level seem to represent the need of humans to formalise events; to create rituals to confer meaning upon, and to control their lives. To fight in the lists before an audience and judges, and according to rules is a quite different activity from fighting like animals. Once more, Theseus, in building the lists, is presented as ordering human life. It is perhaps important that the lists are the product of artists as well as builders for art, like ritual and ceremony, is one of the means by which we invest our lives with meaning. The temples of the gods, then, represent different ways of making sense of the world.

The gods

The gods of the *Knight's Tale* are, of course, the gods of classical myth; Saturn, Jupiter, Mars, Venus, Diana, Juno, Mercury, and so on. In the earlier part of the poem we have been reminded of Juno's hatred of Thebes and of Mercury's killing of Argus, and in Part Three itself, various myths associated with Mars, Venus and Diana are mentioned.

The gods and goddesses also represent the values and desires of the various characters: Theseus as befits a fighter is dedicated to Mars; Emily, who does not want to marry, worships Diana; while Arcite and Palamon respectively worship Mars and Venus: Arcite worships Mars because he believes he will win Emily through victory in battle, Palamon prays to Venus, the goddess of love. The gods can thus represent the meaning of life for individuals, and that way of speaking is still with us when we speak of people worshipping fame or money.

The gods, however, have another aspect, for they also exist as figures for all that is beyond human control, and here their function as planetary forces is important. Mars, Venus, Jupiter, Saturn, and Diana in her connexion with the moon are, of course, planets.

Medieval and classical astronomy pictures the universe with the earth at the centre, enclosed within a series of concentric spheres. A planet is embedded within the wall of each sphere, and each sphere rotates at a different speed. The order of the planets, moving outward from the earth, is the Moon, Mercury, Venus, the Sun, Mars, Jupiter and Saturn. In the outermost, enclosing sphere is the unmoved mover of the universe, the 'First Moevere' of Theseus's final speech, equated in Christian, though not in classical, thought with God.

In Chaucer's time there was no distinction made between astronomy and astrology, and most people believed that in their movements through the heavens the planets exerted some influence on the lives of humans, though the extent of that influence was always debated (this belief is still with us, of course, and many people consult their horoscopes with varying degrees of seriousness). If one believed that men's lives were completely dominated by the stars, then this clearly denied any notion of free will. For this reason astrology was regarded with suspicion by the church; while an orthodox Christian could believe that the planets might affect a man's physical constitution and what happened to him, he had also to believe that they did not influence his free will, his moral being. This is not an entirely easy position to hold, of course, and the question of free will – largely because of philosophical and theological develop- ments – is of considerable importance in the fourteenth century. The planets, then, are a useful device by means of which Chaucer is able to raise new questions about destiny and fate; about the kind of order governing men's lives. His gods are thus complex: planetary forces, powerful mythical personages, and projections of men's deepest desires.

Venus is the first to be described, the decoration of her temple exhibiting her deepest characteristics as they are defined by Theseus. The first pictures we are told about catch the attention just because they are nonvisual, and we are faced with the oddity of trying to imagine paintings of 'broken slepes', 'sikes colde', 'firy strokes of the desirynge . . . '; but then the description moves to something more capable of visual representation, and we meet personifications of various aspects and attributes of love:

> Pleasaunce and Hope, Desir, Foolhardynesse,
> Beautee and Youthe, Bauderie, Richesse,
> Charmes and Force, Lesynges, Flaterye,
> Despense, Bisynesse, and Jalousye,
> That wered of yelewe gooldes a gerland,
> And a cokkow sittynge on hir hand   (1925–30)

This kind of personification, a device by which abstract qualities are presented as human figures, is common in medieval literature and art. Often the connection between the figure and the quality it represents is reinforced by emblematic details. Interestingly, only one figure here, Jealousy, has this kind of detail. She has a garland of marigolds, for yellow is traditionally the colour, and marigold the flower, of jealousy. The cuckoo on her shoulder is an emblem of jealousy because it seems to give rise to that emotion by its habit of laying eggs in other bird's nests. The words 'cuckoo' and 'cuckold' are closely related.

After these personifications the pictures of two different places are described; Mount Citheraeon of classical myth (probably mistaken by Boccaccio, Chaucer's source, for the island Cythera, one of the chief centres of the worship of Venus), and the Garden of Love with its porter, Ydelnesse (an ambiguous word meaning 'folly' as well as 'lack of employment'). This garden is made to recall, and is to some extent modelled upon, the garden of love in the twelfth-century allegory, *The Romance of the Rose*. The garden here, however, and its inhabitants, are much less attractive – and this may be the point of the reference – than those of the *Romance*.

As well as personifications and places associated with Venus there are also depicted the stories of mythical men and women who have been overwhelmed and destroyed by love, and both personifications and representative figures suggest the emotion as destructive rather than attractive: the personifications include enchantments, lying, foolhardiness, flattery, and the stories are on the whole ugly or tragic. Love is called a net, 'a las', a word Theseus has used of it earlier; its power to cause pain emphasised by the rhyme ' . . . a las/ . . . Allas'.

In the midst of the temple stands the statue of Venus, sharply iconographic, and contrasting in its visual effect with most of what has gone before. The waves from which she rises are 'grene, and brighte as any glas', she has 'a rose gerland' and 'dowves flikerynge' around her head, a musical instrument in her hands. Water, doves, roses, musical instruments are all attributes, symbols, or this sea-born goddess; and with her, predictably, is blind Cupid, with his bow and arrows, ready to inspire the most ill-matched with passion.

The description of Mars is considerably longer than that of Venus; its menace, predictably, more clearly stated. Just as the walls of Venus's temple show places particularly associated with her, so in Mars's temple we are given pictures of his temple in Thrace, forbidding, strongly fortified, set in a barren and sinister landscape. Also on the walls, just as in Venus's temple, personified figures are painted, representing attributes of Mars: *Felonye, Ire, Drede, Contek, Meschaunce, Woodnesse*. There are also representative figures under the domination of Mars: the suicide, the hunter, the carter. The connection of some of the figures with Mars is obvious because of their activities; others belong to occupations under the influence of the planetary force.

The different images of destructiveness decorating the temple culminate in the image of Conquest, with a sword poised over his head, typifying the instability of a power based on force. The followers of Mars are not shown in their success, but in their deaths, and this adds to the menace surrounding the god. The sense of fatedness in this passage is extreme, for the slaughtered heroes depicted on the walls of the temple have not been born at this time, we are told; their fate, however, is *depeinted* in the stars, and over the head of Mars, firmly identifying him with the planetary force, are two constellations, Puella and Rubeus, used in predicting the future.

The statue of Mars is armed, grim, mad-looking (and it is worth registering that *woodnesse*, madness, has also been a characteristic of Palamon and Arcite and, indeed, of Theseus). There is paradox here, for the narrator in showing us a mad god seems to erect disorder into a shaping force; seems to show irrationality and loss of control as the dominating feature of the world he has created. The image of the wolf devouring a man at the feet of Mars is effective on two different levels; in one sense it is the animal in man, devouring what is human in him; the triumph of violence over reason (and again we recall that Palamon, Arcite and Theusus have all been likened to wild animals in their anger). More generally, it is an image of sheer destructiveness. It may be, too, an oblique reference to the story of Mars's children, Romulus and Remus, the founders of Rome. If this is so, then the tenderness of the real wolf stands in contrast to the savagery of the symbolic wolf – Mars; set beside the suggestion of Mars destroying his followers is the nurturing of his children in the animal kingdom.

If the temples of Mars and Venus have been presented as embodying the destructiveness of their gods, there is little to suggest that Diana is a kinder deity. The walls of her temple are decorated with pictures of those who have offended against chastity; Acteon who because he saw the naked goddess, was turned into a stag and killed by his own hounds, Callisto, seduced by Jupiter and turned first into a bear, then into a constellation. Daphne, transformed into a laurel as she fled the sexual advances of Apollo, shows a different facet of the worship of the goddess, for her story suggests chastity as self-destructive.

Diana is the goddess of hunting as well as of chastity; as the moon she is also a planetary force and Lucina the goddess of childbirth. In some myths she is equated with Persephone, the wife of Pluto the ruler of the underworld. Her statue suggests all of these aspects, though as it gazes at the woman in childbirth there is no hint of the compassion we might expect of Lucina.

In the representations Theseus has ordered, then, the gods seem cruel and uncaring. At best they preside impassively over various forms of suffering, at worst they activate disaster. Rather than implying an ordered world through them, Theseus seems to have deified disorder.

From the description of the temples, the narrator turns with his usual abruptness to the arrival of Palamon and Arcite in Athens. Predictably the knights whom the lovers have brought with them are outstanding; and the narrator pauses to explain this, ostensibly appealing to our experience of such events:

> Ye knowen wel that every lusty knyght
> That loveth paramours and hath his myght,
> Were it in Engelond or elleswhere,
> They wolde, hir thankes, wilnen to be there, –
> To fighte for a lady, *benedicitee!*
> It were a lusty sighte for to see.   (2111–16)

His bland assumption that everyone is ready to fight for a lady, not only within a story but in real-life England, produces the same kind of mild comic shock as his earlier jokes with the narrative, and serves something of the same purpose. By it we are distanced from Palamon's and Arcite's exercise and invited to view the assumptions of romance with critical detachment. Our knowledge of the pilgrims, the narrator's fictional audience, to whom his appeal is primarily made, brings home to us the more strongly the exclusiveness of the genre's values.

The detailed description of the fourteenth-century armour worn by Palamon's knights continues to bring the world of the story into connection with the England of the pilgrimage. In its reiteration of the construction 'some wol . . . ' the passage draws attention to itself, and the anachronism of its information is stressed 'Ther is no newe gyse that it nas old' (2125).

Central to Palamon's company of knights is Lygurge, the king of Thrace. The description dwells upon his strength and splendour. At first the emphasis is on his striking appearance, on his glowing strangely-coloured eyes:

> They gloweden bitwixen yelow and reed,
> And lik a grifphon looked he aboute.   (2132–3)

The catalogue of his limbs – muscles, shoulders, arms – stresses his strength, which is also suggested metonymically through his possessions, through the bulls pulling his chariot and the bear skin he wears.

The whiteness of the bulls and of the great, richly-adorned dogs around him; the bear skin 'col-blak for old' with its 'nayles yelewe and brighte as any gold'; his hair, black 'as any ravenes fethere' have a strong visual appeal. At the same time, the detail of his hair introduces a note of threat, for the raven conventionally in medieval heroic literature is the bird that scavenges on the battle field.

Emetrius's description is placed beside that of Lygurge, and again the emphasis is on his power and exotic splendour. Once more, the animals which surround him, and to which he is compared, enforce his strength and ferocity; tame lions and leopards, an 'egle tame' on his wrist. He himself 'as a leon . . . his lookyng caste'. Where the colours used to describe Lygurge are black and gold and white, Emetrius is predominantly golden, from his hair to the animals which surround him. The other touches of colour are the red and white of the rubies and pearls which decorate his mantle.

The physical descriptions of the two champions suggest them as Saturnalian and Martian figures, the character and physical appearance of each as having been influenced by the planet in the ascendant at their birth. Thus, even in the most ceremonious activities men devise, the influence of the planets makes itself felt.

After the extended descriptions of the two champions the narrator outlines briefly, using the familar device of *occupatio*, the arrangements for their entertainment 'Of al this make I now no mencioun' (2206).

He then describes the visits of the lovers and Emily to the temples of their respective gods. Once more we are made aware that these gods are also planetary forces as each goes to pray at the hour of the day in which their particular planet has most influence.

Palamon prays in the temple of Venus that the goddess of love will grant his prayers. He describes his love as pain and torment; as hell. Despite the fact that he does not pray for victory in the tournament – 'I ne axe nat tomorwe to have victorie' – and professes himself to be without interest in arms or the renown which fighting brings, he still uses metaphors of war as he speaks of his love and promises to 'holden werre alwey with chastitee'. Since Emily worships Diana, the goddess of chastity, his language, despite its conventionality, betrays the aggression inherent in his idea of love; an aggression which emerges further in his prayer 'I wolde have fully possessioun/Of Emilye . . . '. Emily is thus reduced by him to the equivalent of the spoils of battle. Notice, too, that Palamon prays for death if Arcite is successful; a reminiscence of his pleas to Theseus when he and Arcite are discovered fighting.

After some delay the statue of Venus signals that Palamon's love will be successful, thus foreshadowing the eventual outcome of the story. However, rather like the lovers in earlier scenes where they stress so insistently the unpredictability of their lives, the reader is left in some uncertainty, for the narrator does not commit himself to the truthfulness of the sign, but contents himself with telling us that Palamon believes in it:

> For thogh the signe shewed a delay,
> Yet wiste he wel that graunted was his boone.   (2268–9)

The prayers of Emily are set between those of Palamon and Arcite. This departure from the order in which the temples have been described serves, perhaps, to accentuate the way in which she has come between the lovers.

As we hear Emily's voice for the first time we become aware of her as being more than the object of Palamon's and Arcite's passion. In contrast with his descriptions of Palamon's and Arcite's prayers the narrator focuses upon the circumstances surrounding those of Emily; upon the maidens she takes with her, the preparations they make:

> Ful redily with hem the fyr they hadde,
> The'encens, the clothes, and the remenant al
> That to the sacrifice longen shal   (2276–8)

The sense of elaborate ritual is increased rather than dispelled by his somewhat prurient 'But hou she dide her ryte I dar nat telle' (2284).

In his concentration upon the externals of the scene the narrator adopts a rather similar position to that of the two lovers, establishing Emily as a desirable figure rather than as a character with her own desires. The perspective changes sharply, however, when Emily speaks, praying to be released from the necessity of loving either suitor. To her marriage is servitude, chastity freedom. The image of Emily serving Diana as a huntress is poignant and establishes her as the one necessary and helpless sufferer in the tale:

> I am, thow woost, yet of thy compaignye,
> A mayde, and love huntynge and venerye,
> And for to walken in the wodes wilde,
> And noght to ben a wyf and be with childe.
> Noght wol I knowe compaignye of man.   (2307–11)

Despite the way in which the narrator has distanced us at times from the lovers, we have probably up to this point acquiesced in their sense of helplessness in the face of an unkind fate. Now, however, Emily emerges as the helpless victim of their desires. Her fate seems to be not so much the work of the gods as of their love for her, a love which with all its humility is careless, indeed unconscious, of her wishes. The lovers do not ask for her consent, her 'grace', but for that of Theseus and the gods. In this their love could be described as quite uncourtly according to literary conventions, but such negotiations for marriage are not too far removed from fourteenth-century realities.

In answer to Emily's prayer, a sign is given once more, and once more the sign foreshadows the outcome of the tale. One fire on the altar goes out, and after a while relights; the other is extinguished completely, its wood dripping 'as it were blody dropes'. Unlike the lovers Emily is unable to understand the portent, and as she weeps Diana appears in order to tell her that her marriage is ordained, 'by eterne word written and confermed'.

As with that of Palamon in the temple of Venus, so the description of Arcite in the temple of Mars is almost entirely confined to his prayer. Just as Palamon has reminded Venus of her love for Adonis, so Arcite recalls Mars's love for Venus, and his entrapment in the net Vulcan, Venus's husband, threw over them in order to exhibit them to the mockery of the other gods. Vulcan's *las* recalls earlier uses of the word by Theseus and Arcite to describe the power of love.

Like Palamon, Arcite insists on the suffering of love, both that of Mars and his own. Love is 'peyne', 'hoote fir'. He emphasises his own vulnerability by speaking of his youth'; he is 'yong and unkonnynge' and love has 'offended' him. However, like Palamon's, his language betrays the aggression underlying his devotion 'I moot with strengthe wynne hire in the place' (2399). Although his words refer ostensibly to the tournament, they suggest, in the context of Emily's desire not to marry, something approaching rape. Like Palamon again, Arcite promises perpetual worship to his god, and like Palamon, though more equivocally, he is promised victory.

As Arcite prays to win the tournament we may remember his earlier lamentation that prayer is dangerous because of men's inability to foresee the consequences of answered prayers, but this connection perhaps only becomes fully obvious later in the poem with Saturn's speech. Though he does not get what he wants, Arcite, just as much as Palamon, gets what he prays for, and the homeliness of the image conveying his state of mind as he leaves the temple adds to the irony of his situation:

> Arcite anon unto his in is fare,
> As fayn as fowel is of the brighte sonne.

(2436–7)

After the description of the splendid lists and the orderly, ceremonious prayers in the temples we move from the characters' perception of the gods to what actually goes on in the heavens, which is far less dignified; Venus and Mars squabble over the outcome of the battle, and significantly it is not Jupiter, the ordering, benign god who can settle the dispute, but Saturn, the unfortunate planet, the planet causing disaster and mishap, who intervenes.

Saturn in his description of his workings defines himself as a planetary force:

> 'My cours, that hath so wyde for to turne,
> Hath moore power than woot any man.'

(2454–5)

Saturn, of course, is the planet furthest from the earth, and therefore with the longest journey to make in its revolutions. His planetary status is further suggested with his reference to dwelling in 'the signe of the Leoun'. The power and terror of Saturn emerges forcefully in his description of the devastation he brings about. The reiteration of 'Myn is . . . ' at the beginning of so many lines is reinforced by the repetition of verbal nouns: *drenchyng, stranglyng, hangyng, groynnynge, empoysonyng,* until it seems as though there is nothing that will escape him. Although Saturn seems to claim a monopoly on disasters some seem to belong to him with a particular fitness in being brought about unwittingly by their victims:

> The fallynge of the toures and of the walles
> Upon the mynour or the carpenter.

(2464–5)

Although Saturn is presented on one level as an alternative to Mars, another unfortunate planet, his operations recall very strongly the activities of the other as they are depicted on the walls of his temple 'The cook yscalded, for al his longe ladel' (2020) and 'The cartere overryden with his carte' (2022). Thus, the two possibilities for ordering the outcome of the tale are seen as almost equally destructive, and equally careless of human intentions. The lack of any principle of order in the heavens is stressed by the fact that Saturn produces an *ad hoc* solution, just to please his grand-daughter,

Venus. Diana's mention of the 'eterne word' of the gods seems singularly inappropriate to describe Saturn's improvisation.

Part IV (Robinson, I 2483–3107)

The tournament is described at length, and we see Arcite struck down in his moment of triumph by the Fury Saturn has sent. After a brief account of the aftermath of the tournament, Arcite's physical condition is described in detail, and we turn to his dying speech in which he movingly commends Palamon to Emily. The description of his funeral, one of the great set-pieces of the tale follows, and the work ends with Theseus's assertion of a divine order, and the marriage of Emily to Palamon.

The events of the day before the tournament are dealt with in no more than five lines, and the festivities 'in Venus heigh servyse' (for both knights are fighting for love) receive a bare mention. Our attention is then directed to the bustle and 'claterynge' of the following morning as those who are to fight make their preparations. The narrator describes little in close detail, but evokes the scene by a catalogue of the adornments and the accoutrements of the knights, and then details those engaged in preparation for the fight. The activity and movement of the scene is suggested by quick switches from one thing to another and the listing of activities all are concerned with. The list of participles – *nailynge, bokelynge, giggynge, lacynge* – gives a sense of bustling, purposeful occupation, while references to 'goldsmythrye', 'sheeldes brighte', 'gold-hewen helmes' invest the scene with glamour.

Much technical language is used, and the passage has something of the air of a medieval equivalent of a football commentary; it seems designed to appeal to those who know all about the fine points of tournaments. The noise of the scene is evoked by the listing of the musical instruments 'That in the bataille blowen blody sounes' (2512). We are given, too, a sense of the audience's involvement through the repetition of 'Somme seyden . . . ' 'Somme helden . . . ' 'Somme with . . . ' 'Somme seyde . . . '. After this picture of relentless movement the narrator turns to Theseus and his part in the events. Theseus's regal power is emphasised; he is 'the grete Theseus', 'duc Theseus', and 'Arrayed right as he were a god in trone' (2529). These descriptions are given weight by the actions of the people, who press forward to see him and 'doon heigh reverence'. As he sits at a window looking down on those below his will is made known by a herald in terms that confer on him an almost divine status 'The lord hath of his heigh discrecioun . . . ' (2537). The phrases 'to shapen' and 'his firste purpos modifye' enchance this suggestion, as does the reaction of the people 'God save swich a lord, that is so good' (2563).

The edicts which Theseus lays down to prevent maiming and killing are reported in detail, and paradoxically the listing of the weapons that are to be used and not used increases our sense of the bloodiness of the whole affair.

After instructions for the fight have been laid down the contenders, one on either side of Theseus, and followed by Hippolyta and Emily, and then the rest of the company, ride ceremoniously to the lists.

When the audience is seated Arcite, as is fitting, rides into the lists through the gateway beneath the temple of Mars, and Palamon through that beneath the temple of Venus. Their equality is carefully stressed.

The description of the tournament is yet another of the tale's set-pieces. Its heavy alliteration enforces the fierceness of the struggle:

> Out brest the blood with stierne stremes rede;
> With myghty maces the bones they tobreste.
>
> (2610–11)

At the same time, the disconnectedness of the fighting is conveyed by the grammatical patterns which establish themselves in the lines. The grammatical structure of preposition + verb (an inversion of the normal pattern) – 'Up spryngen . . . ', 'Out brest . . . ' – which occurs at the beginning of so many lines is interspersed with that of pronoun + verb – 'He rolleth . . . ', 'He foyneth . . . ', and variants upon both constructions. This pattern is reinforced by the absence of connectives such as *and*.

It is only after the fighting has been described at length that Arcite and Palamon are mentioned; as in their earlier fight they are compared with wild animals, and once more the parallelism is maintained between them; Arcite is like a tiger whose cub has been stolen, Palamon like a 'fel leon'. Once more their savagery and *woodness* is stressed, and – despite Theseus's commands – once more 'Out renneth blood on bothe hir sydes rede' (2635).

The tone changes with the line 'Som tyme an ende ther is of every dede' (2636), and we are given a fairly unemotional account of Palamon's capture. In order to give lustre to the lovers it is emphasised that their two outstanding champions are bested. Palamon is conquered, not by superior skill, but by sheer weight of numbers. The tournament is brought to an end by Theseus who declares with certainty, and of course wrongly, 'Arcite of Thebes shal have Emelie' (2658).

After a short, hyperbolic description of the joy of the crowd, the tale moves to the heavens where Venus cries with rage over the defeat of her servant; with her we are left to await the outcome of Saturn's prediction that all will go according to her wishes. Meanwhile, below on earth the ceremonies of victory have begun. The emphasis here is all on sound, on

> The trompours with the *loude* mynstralcie;
> The heraudes, that *ful loude* yelle and crie,
>
> (2671–2)

Characteristically the narrator holds up the action, mixing the levels of narration by his assumption that *his* audience is behaving in the same way as the audience of the tournament 'But herkneth me, and stynteth noyse a lite' (2674).

The image of Arcite as he parades in triumph through the lists is pictorial and emblematic:

> This fierse Arcite hath of his helm ydon,
> And on a courser, for to shewe his face,
> He priketh endelong the large place   (2676–8)

At the same time, the narrator's generalisation that women 'folwen alle the favour of Fortune' distances us from the general rejoicing so that we wonder a little about the 'freendlich ye' that Emily casts on Arcite.

At the moment of Arcite's triumph his horse stumbles, he falls on his head, and his chest is crushed. The accident is presented as the work of Saturn who has pressed Pluto the god of the underworld into his service. The description of the accident is factual, detailed, strangely prosaic, and Arcite's new state contrasts sharply with his earlier splendour:

> As blak he lay as any cole or crowe,
> So was the blood yronnen in his face.   (2692–3)

Arcite is carried to his bed, with all assuming that he will live, and the arrangements for comforting and entertaining the contenders are described. As Theseus has decreed, none is slain, and yet the narrator dwells on the wounds they have received and on the remedies needed to cure them rather than on the feasting and general rejoicing. There is a strange prolixity about this passage, almost a suggestion of reported speech, as if we hear the verdict of Theseus's court 'For soothly ther was no disconfiture . . . ' (2721), even as the reasons for possible discomfiture are suggested. The ostensible purpose of the passage is to insist that the contenders have all fought bravely and deserve honour, but the details of what has befallen them emphasise more forcibly the violence of the event. 'Of this bataille I wol namoore endite' (2741). The narrator with his usual signal moves back to Palamon and Arcite. It is noticeable that he continues to bracket them together, even though it is on Arcite's speech that he concentrates.

Through the description of Arcite's physical state we are once more made aware of the fragility of men, and the glamour of fighting is qualified by the hideousness of the broken body. The language in which Arcite's condition is described is medical and technical. According to medieval medical theory the body works through a force called *virtus*. There are three kinds of *virtus*: *virtus naturalis* which is concerned with the liver; *virtus spiritualis* or *vitalis* which works through the heart, and the *virtus animalis*, operating through the brain. Breathing, a function of the *virtus animalis*, is necessary to regulate the heat of the body. The *virtus animalis* feels what is poisonous to the *virtus naturalis* and works to expel it. Arcite's wounds are such that the *virtus animalis* cannot work to maintain the body's proper activities. The narrator concludes his detailed medical report with the flippant comment 'Fare wel physik! go ber the man to chirche!' (2760). Arcite is thus reduced in this description to his physicality; seen as a kind of machine, helpless as the cogs refuse to work.

By contrast, his dying speech is poignant, its language controlled, ceremonious, rhetorical. Its repetitions, inversions and apostrophes mark it as poetic high style:

> Allas, the deeth! allas, myn Emelye!
> Allas, departynge of oure compaignye!
> Allas, myn hertes queene! allas, my wyf!   (2773–5)

Arcite speaks of his coming death, reminding Emily of his *wo*, of the 'peynes stronge' he has suffered for her. Emily is his 'hertes lady'; she is also 'endere of my lyf'. His language recalls the conventional metaphors of courtly love which he and Palamon have used earlier in the tale, but ironically he now speaks no more than the literal, painful, truth.

Arcite turns from Emily to the world itself, and again we are reminded of his state earlier in the tale, for his questions recall poignantly those he has already so repeatedly asked. Death now provides him with an answer as he contemplates the loneliness of the grave:

> What is this world? what asketh men to have?
> Now with his love, now in his colde grave
> Allone, withouten any compaignye.   (2777–9)

He then turns to the living, transcending his rivalry with Palamon as he recommends him to Emily, and returns finally to those values which his love has made him forget:

> That is to seyen, trouthe, honour, knyghthede,
> Wysdom, humblesse, estaat, and heigh kynrede,
> Fredom, and al that longeth to that art –   (2789–91)

On one level his words can be taken as asserting the importance of a human order to which men subdue their individual wishes. However, despite their dignity, they are disquieting, for he describes Palamon in a list of attributes in which his high birth and his virtues are not differentiated, but presented as equally important, as amounting to the same thing. 'That art' in the final, summarising clause seems an inappropriate heading under which to include 'estaat and heigh kynrede'. This inappropriateness may make us wonder also about the sense in which Palamon *serveth* Emily. Thus, while Arcite on his deathbed affirms aristocratic values, the terms in which he does so do not necessarily establish those values as being equally compelling for the reader.

After this speech the processes of death are described briefly, and the narrator abandons Arcite. There is a note of grim, dismissive humour in his agnosticism about his hero's fate in the next world.

The narrator then says he will 'speken forth of Emelye', but, as usual, Emily gets little attention. The tone is dismissive, ironic at her expense and that of women as a class, as he generalises ' . . . wom-

men have such sorwe . . . '. Women are to be idealised and treated
as sovereign; they may be the occasion for displays of chivalric skill,
and yet there is a half-resentful suggestion that they are of coarser
grain than men, and unlike them will not be destroyed by love. The
whole description of the universal mourning has a touch of distancing
comedy about it, with the verbs *shrighte* and *howleth* suggesting
Palamon's and Emily's grief as rather less than dignified. The
association of wealth and love, too, seems comically inappropriate to
the occasion:

> 'Why woldestow be deed,' thise wommen crye,
> 'And haddest gold ynough, and Emelye?'   (2835–6)

This movement towards the mock-heroic is punctured bathetically
by Aegeus's speech, reputedly the only thing which can comfort
Theseus. In one way he offers irreproachably common-place consolation 'This world nys but a thurghfare ful of wo' (2847). However, the
obviousness of his opening remark may suggest his consolation as
rather threadbare:

> 'Right as ther dyed nevere man,' quod he,
> 'That he ne lyvede in erthe in some degree,
> Right so ther lyvede never man,' he seyde,
> 'In al this world, that som tyme he ne deyde.'
>
>   (2842–5)

The whole of Aegeus's speech fits emotionally with Palamon's and
Arcite's perceptions throughout the poem, but leaves us with a sense
of unalleviated bleakness.

After Aegeus's gloom comes Theseus's new attempt to make some
sense of the accidents of life. Just as the tournament is held in the
grove where Palamon and Arcite first fight so too is the funeral,
described in a set-piece as lavish as the ceremony itself. The funeral
pyre is prepared and Arcite's richly-dressed body laid upon it. Once
more the mourning is stressed. Palamon is there 'With flotery berd
and ruggy, asshy heeres,' (2883), and Emily is 'The rewefulleste of al
the compaignye' (2886). The pageantry of the funeral recalls that of
the tournament. Once more there is a procession, and once more the
richness of the scene is brought to our attention. The horses bearing
Arcite's arms are 'trapped . . . in steel al gliterynge', they are 'grete

and white', the case of Arcite's bow is of 'brend gold'. The description of the rites is detailed; Theseus carries vessels 'Al ful of hony, milk, and blood, and wyn' (2908), and Emily comes 'with fyr in honde'. The size of the pyre is carefully given, and the trees used in its construction suggested by the device of *occupatio*, which the narrator uses here to give an effect of overwhelming extravagance without committing himself to a realistic account:

> But how the fyr was maked upon highte,
> Ne eek the names that the trees highte,
> As ook, firre, birch, aspe, alder, holm, popler,
> . . .
> . . . ne kepe I nat to seye.   (2919–60)

The devastated grove is endowed with feeling and consciousness; the ground itself 'That was nat wont to seen the sonne brighte' (2932), is *agast*. This, together with the listing of the trees, and of the gods and animals deprived of their habitations, suggests the destructiveness of the ceremony Theseus has ordered, and recalls the devastation following his conquest of Thebes.

The passage in which the funeral is described is one of extended *occupatio*, arranged in one long sentence stretching for over forty lines, 'But how . . . ne keepe I nat to seye.' Within it the narrator lists all the things he is not going to describe; the line-openings, 'Ne how . . . ', 'Ne what . . . ', are characteristic. Frequently he takes two or three lines in *not* describing some of these features, and the length of one of these 'non-descriptions' is emphasised by a new pattern of parallel line-openings; 'And then . . . '

After this account of the funeral, the narrator promises to be brief, to 'maken of my longe tale an ende', and slides over an unspecified number of years into the parliament called by Theseus. A note of vagueness enters as its circumstances are described; 'Thanne semed me . . . ', 'upon certein pointz and caas'. The parliament is the occasion of Theseus's great assertion of order, and of the marriage of Palamon and Emily; its point, however, is political, to gain 'fully of Thebans obeisaunce'.

Theseus, once more, makes ceremony out of his political priorities, speaking with 'sad visage' (although *sad* has something of its modern meaning here, it bears the primary sense of 'solemn', 'ceremonious').

Setting aside the unruly planetary gods, Theseus invokes the *First Moevere*, asserting the control of that being over the whole of his creation. Everything is held in its proper place, bound by 'the faire cheyne of love'; all that is born in this 'wrecched world' has its allotted span of time which, although it may be cut short, can never be extended. From 'this ordre' we are able to infer the wholeness and perfection of its creator who, in 'his wise purveiaunce', has ordained that one generation must succeed another.

Theseus then illustrates the inevitability of dissolution in a long list of examples, concluding that it is folly to rebel against the divine order, wisdom 'To maken vertu of necessitee' (3042). If death is inevitable, then Arcite has been fortunate, for it is better for a man:

> To dyen in his excellence and flour . . .
> Than whan his name appalled is for age.
>
> (3048–53)

He concludes his speech by saying that the time for mourning is over, and tells Emily that he wishes her to marry Palamon, her 'owene knyght' and 'a kynges brother sone' 'That serveth yow with wille herte, and myght' (3078).

Theseus begins the speech on an expository and rational note. His urge to define and demonstrate is expressed in clauses qualifying his central statements: 'Al mowe they yet . . . ', 'For it is preeved . . . ', 'And therfore . . . '. The philosophical tone of the passage is further enforced by the abstract vocabulary; words like *sentence, corrumpable, ordinaunce, duracioun* are frequent, and give weight to Theseus's assertions. However, although his purpose is to stress the orderliness of the divine dispensation he describes, perhaps what emerges most strongly is its power. The elements 'may nat flee' beyond their bounds, men 'may nat pace' beyond their appointed day of death in this 'wrecched world adoun'. In this context 'the feyre cheyne of love' bears some resemblance to Palamon's and Arcite's fetters during their imprisonment, or to 'loves laas' in which they have also been bound. Theseus's much later reference to 'this foule prisoun of this lif' heightens the similarity.

For Theseus, death is the real manifestation of divine power, and his tone changes as he moves away from abstract argument to dwell upon the inevitable destruction of all created things. The bleakness of the picture he paints is enforced by the range of examples he gives: *ook, stoon, ryver, tounes* will all, we are repetitively reminded, decay 'Yet at the laste wasted . . . ' (3020), 'Yet wasteth it . . . ' (3023), ' . . . se we wante and wende.' (3025).

Theseus then insists on the inevitability of human death through a series of oppositions: *man/womman, youthe/age, kyng/page.* Unlike the decay of the physical world, however, death is arbitrary and unpredictable. Just as it strikes in youth as well as age, so it may come in any place, in *bed*, *sea*, *feeld*, and the adjectives *depe*, *wide*, together with the repetition of 'Som in . . . ' suggest the world as cold and inhospitable. Theseus's summing up 'Ther helpeth noght, al goth that ilke weye' (3033), is given weight, not only by the preceding desolate lines, but by his flat repetition 'al this thyng moot deye'

After this contemplation of worldly transience, Theseus's conclusion that it is folly to rebel against 'Juppiter, the kyng' (whom he treats as synonymous with the First Mover) seems inescapable. The consolation he offers, so briefly mentioned, that all returns to Jupiter, the 'propre welle' from which it has originated, may not, however, seem quite so compelling, for there is little or nothing within the speech to give it imaginative force.

How far we accept the comfort he finds in the manner of Arcite's death may well depend on what we choose to emphasise. Persuaded by the vocabulary of chivalry: *honour*, *excellence*, *flour*, we may be moved to agree that

> certeinly a man hath moost honour
> To dyen in his excellence and flour,
> Whan he is siker of his goode name;　　　(3047–9)

We may reflect, however, that this consolation cannot be found in every death; that many die when their reputations are 'apalled . . . for age'. If so, then we may question the value of the order which Theseus discerns in 'this foule prisoun of this lyf'.

The rest of Theseus's speech engineers the conventional happy ending of romance as he consigns Emily to Palamon's arms. Because of its conventionality we are likely to accept it at face value, but again we may be tempted to question the 'parfit joy' of the union and, indeed, to question the reality of Palamon's former 'service' to Emily; a 'service' which has been questioned within the tale.

The narrator, however, seems exempt from this kind of doubt:

> For now is Palamon in alle wele,
> Lyvynge in blisse, in richesse, and in heele
>
> 　　　　　　　　　　　　　　　　　　(3101–2)

5 CHAUCER AND BOCCACCIO

Chaucer borrowed the story of Palamon and Arcite from Boccaccio, a rather older contemporary. He may have come upon Boccaccio's work, the *Teseida*, on one of his visits to Italy, and it is even possible that he met Boccaccio in 1372–3.

Boccaccio was one of the leading Italian writers of his day and, like Dante and Petrarch, those other great Italian poets of the period – like Chaucer himself, indeed – he did much to make his own language one in which serious subjects could be treated. He was also fascinated by the languages and literature of ancient Greece and Rome, and was part of a growing movement to recover and translate the works of classical authors.

Boccaccio's *Teseida* models itself on the classical epic. Like the epic it has twelve books, invocations to the Muses, an elaborate style making great use of extended similes, and treats the heroic world of Greek myth. Theseus (Teseo in Boccaccio's version), the gods, and many of the characters and stories mentioned in the *Teseida* would have been familiar to medieval readers who knew their classical authors. However, the story of Palemone and Arcita seems to have been Boccaccio's own invention, despite his claim that it is a very old story.

Boccaccio's work is nearly four times as long as Chaucer's but the *Knight's Tale* is not merely a summary of the *Teseida* , for while Chaucer omits some episodes and condenses others ruthlessly, he expands others, and even adds some of his own. His changes produce a quite different work, and a comparison of the two versions helps to bring out some of the distinctive qualities of the *Knight's Tale*.

THE *TESEIDA*

Book I

After an elaborate opening Boccaccio introduces his main characters, Palemone and Arcita. He then gives an account of Theseus's conquest of the Amazons which is presented as an act of retaliation rather than aggression, and of his marriage to Hippolyta. Plans for a marriage betwen Emilia and Theseus's cousin Acates are outlined.

Book II

After an account of Creon's tyranny and his hatred of the Greeks, Theseus's homecoming and his meeting with the mourning women is described at length. Creon's refusal to allow the bodies of their husbands to be buried is presented as an act of cruelty rather than disrespect, for until the bodies are buried their souls will be unable to enter the underworld.

Theseus sets out against Thebes, kills Creon and returns to the women the bodies of their husbands. After the battle the bodies of Palemone and Arcita are discovered, not by pillagers, but by Greeks looking for their dead, and are brought with great respect before Theseus. Despite their disdain Theseus treats them well, and debates carefully what to do with them, afraid that if he frees them they will make war against him. He imprisons them for life but, unlike Chaucer's Theseus, gives them a room in the palace and everything they need.

Book III

We are told of the despair of Palemone and Arcita, and of their first sight of Emilia, whom they see after they have been imprisoned for nearly a year. By contrast, Chaucer extends the length of time they suffer 'This passeth yeer by yeer and day by day.' (1033).

In the *Teseida* it is Arcita who sees Emilia first, and the cousins do not quarrel over her, but console one another. Emilia, moreover, hears Palemone's sighs and is pleased at the impression she has created. She visits the garden frequently, taking care to look attractive, and enjoys rousing the desire of the captives.

Pirithous visits Athens, and after a brief description of the two lovers, given when Pirithous visits them in prison, we learn of Arcita's release. The book ends with the laments of the lovers as they take leave of one another. Both are despairing, but their speeches have none of the bitterness against one another that we find in the *Knight's Tale*. Although they see themselves as being in hands of fortune, neither questions the will of the gods.

Book IV

Arcita, after extensive travels, decides to return to Athens when he learns that Emilia's prospective husband has died. He has already changed his name to Pentheus, not Philostratus as in Chaucer, and believes his appearance has altered enough for him to avoid recognition. Boccaccio has no account of an illness of the kind that Chaucer describes, though Emilia, who recognises him immediately, comments on the change in his appearance. Arcita/Pentheus becomes the trusted servant of Theseus, and continues to love Emilia. In the *Teseida* Arcita visits the grove regularly, to sleep and to complain about his unhappy love. His complaints are overheard by Palemone's servant, who tells his master of them. There is thus much less stress on the workings of fate in Boccaccio than in Chaucer.

Book V

When he learns of Arcita's return Palemone determines to escape, and Boccaccio gives a fairly detailed account of the means he uses before describing his meeting in the grove with Arcita. After the two have greeted each other lovingly and told their adventures, Palemone insists, despite Arcita's arguments, on fighting over Emilia. Arcita sees the coming duel as being caused by Juno's hatred of Thebes, and recalls the myth of the foundation of the city, in which the dragon's teeth which Cadmus planted grew into armed men and destroyed one another. After recalling other disasters which befell his ancestors he goes for armour, and the two fight, though without the frenzy of Chaucer's lovers. Neither does Palemone betray Arcita when Theseus discovers them.

After hearing their stories, Theseus forgives the lovers, for he too has been in love. In his speech there are no such puncturing comments as are made in the *Knight's Tale* about Emily's unawareness. Theseus arranges that the lovers should return in a year, each with a hundred companions, to fight in the amphitheatre (already built) for Emilia.

Book VI

The book opens with a summary of Fortune's treatment of the lovers, then the arrival of their supporters in Athens is described. Lycurgus, on Arcita's side, is mentioned, and then other famous heroes are listed. There is no mention of Emetrius, nor is Lycurgus described in detail. The book closes with a description of the celebrations before the tournament.

Book VII

This book takes us up to the opening of the tournament. Theseus addresses the combatants and restricts the weapons to be used: since there is no deadly hatred between the rivals the contest should be friendly. He then institutes himself as judge, and is acclaimed for his desire to protect life. Arcita and Palemone pick their supporters, and on the day before the tournament both pray to their gods.

In Boccaccio's version there is no description of the temples in the lists. Instead, the prayers of the lovers are personified and make their way to the dwelling places of their gods. Arcita's prayer travels to Thrace and finds itself in the kind of scene depicted on the walls of Chaucer's temple of Mars. Boccaccio's Mars, however, is primarily a god of war, and Chaucer extends the description to suggest him as a planetary force, including representatives of occupations under his patronage, and calamities brought about by his influence as an unfortunate planet. The lines from 'The toun destroyed . . . ' to the end of the description are entirely Chaucer's. He also make Boccaccio's description more concrete and vivid; thus Madness becomes 'Woodnesse, laughynge in his rage', and 'The shepne bren- nynge . . . ' is a Chaucerian addition.

Summoned by Arcita's prayer, Boccaccio's Mars visits the temple where his follower is praying and promises him victory by the signs we find in Chaucer.

Boccaccio's Palemone does not confine his attentions to Venus, but visits every other temple in Athens first. Like Arcita's, Palemo- ne's prayer wings its way to his god, this time to Mount Cithaeron, the home of Venus. Boccaccio describes in some detail the beautiful scenery, the grass, birds singing, the small animals, and the music that fills the place. The personifications which surround Venus are on the whole more mixed in Boccaccio than in Chaucer and include Grace, Elegance, Friendliness, and Courtesy, as well as the more suspect qualities in Chaucer's version. In the centre of Boccaccio's garden- like scene lies Venus's temple, adorned, as it is in Chaucer, with depictions – though Boccaccio has a rather different selection – of famous lovers. Venus herself is in the innermost place in her temple, in darkness, half-naked, beautiful, and guarded by riches. Ceres (the goddess of the harvest) and Bacchus (the god of wine) are her attendants. Although Boccaccio's Venus seems less harmful than Chaucer's, Boccaccio's explanations of the symbolism of his description emphasise her destructiveness. Like Mars, Venus visits the temple where Palamone is praying and promises that he will gain his desires.

As in Chaucer, Mars and Venus quarrel, but in the *Teseida* they find their own means of settling their differences, though at this point we are not told how they will do so.

Boccaccio then describes the rites that Emilia performs, though without the touch of prurience Chaucer's narrator displays. Emilia prays to remain a maiden for a little while longer, not as in the *Knight's Tale* for all her life. In Boccaccio she is also fearful of Diana's vengeance if she marries, and sympathetic towards the plight of the lovers; both seem so pleasing that she cannot choose between them, so she prays that the one who loves her most will win. The omens she sees are substantially the same as those in Chaucer.

After a brief account of Emilia's unhappiness and the tension of the lovers, Boccaccio (much later in the story than Chaucer), describes the amphitheatre and the entry of the spectators and combatants.

Book VIII

Boccaccio describes the battle with great elaboration, though, unlike Chaucer, he concentrates on a series of single combats rather than the whole scene. The reactions of the spectators are also described, and Emilia blames her beauty for creating dissension between the lovers. As Arcita begins to triumph she falls deeply in love with him, and ceases to worry about Palemone.

Book IX

Here we learn of Mars's and Venus's solution to their dispute (Saturn is absent from the *Teseida*); Arcita is allowed to win the contest, Palemone eventually to win Emilia. Venus descends to the kingdom of Dis (the Greek equivalent of Pluto) and summons the fury which causes Arcita's horse to shy. Despite his injuries Arcita is able to ride in triumph to Athens, accompanied by Emilia, and by the despairing Palemone and his men.

Before the feast to celebrate Arcita's victory Theseus makes a speech about the workings of Providence, suggesting that if everything is predestined it is useless for men to struggle against their fate. Emilia and Arcita are married, despite the latter's wounds.

Book X

After a description of the funerals of those killed in the tournament we are returned to Arcita whose wounds are pronounced to be incurable, though without any detailed description of his state such as we find in Chaucer. Arcita, recognising that he is near death, asks Theseus that Palemone should marry Emilia; he then laments to Palemone the enmity of Juno against their family and asks him to marry Emilia. When Emilia appears he makes the same plea to her, though without invoking the chivalric values of Chaucer's Arcite, and mourns his approaching death in terms quite similar to those used by Chaucer's hero.

Book XI

In contrast with Chaucer's version, there is no uncertainty about Arcita's fate after his death; his soul is transported to the eighth sphere, and from there he smiles down on the futility of men's lives.

In Athens there is general mourning for him and Aegeus offers Palemone (not Theseus) words of consolation, though these words are not reported. Arcita's pyre is built, and his funeral is described. The detail of this description is copied closely by Chaucer, who omits only a lament by Emilia and a description of the scenes decorating the temple built by Palemone on the place where the pyre has been.

Book XII

Here Boccaccio describes Palemone's marriage to Emilia. Unlike Chaucer, he has the marriage take place immediately after the *days* of mourning are over, and not several *years* later; nor is there any mention of a truce between Athens and Thebes.

Palemone, summoned by Theseus, but not knowing why, is led to Emilia, and Theseus makes a long speech, the equivalent to his 'First Mover' speech in Chaucer. Boccaccio's version, however, is significantly different, beginning with the lines Chaucer assigns to Aegeus:

'Right so ther lyvede never man . . . '. These are followed by the equivalent to the lines in Chaucer beginning 'Loo the ook . . . '.

After the speech Palemone and Emilia, instead of remaining silent, voice their objections to the marriage: Palemone does not want to be disloyal to Arcita, and Emilia fears the vengeance of Diana on her lover. Theseus reassures them, and the preparations for the marriage are described. Boccaccio then describes Emilia's beauty in detail; the marriage takes place, and the story ends with an account of the celebrations, and the joys of the marriage night.

This fairly lengthy summary of the *Teseida* should give you some opportunity to think about the significance of the changes Chaucer makes to its story.

Comparison of the two works helps to emphasise the extreme symmetry of the *Knight's Tale*, and at the same time, the randomness and disorder of the world it describes. Just as Chaucer alters Boccaccio's already very formal work in order to make characters, speeches, events parallel one another even more closely, so he increases the suffering and helplessness of the characters whose actions and emotions are much less motivated, much more arbitrary than those of Boccaccio. These arbitrary characters, who fall in love so suddenly and suffer so deeply, live also in an arbitrary world from which they are able to wrest little meaning, and which is governed by gods representing misfortune and accident as ruling principles. The symmetry of Chaucer's story is thus made to emphasise the chaos of the world it describes.

At the same time, the detail of Chaucer's narration works to distance us both from the characters and from the narrator's perspective on events. We are constantly reminded, either by jokes in the narrative or by the extensive use of *occupatio*, that what we are reading is a fiction, created by the narrator, for *occupatio*, as well as being a useful device for summarising a long story, also draws attention to its user's activity in selecting what he will speak of. Chaucer's changes thus produce a work which inculcates in its readers a much more detached, questioning attitude than the *Teseida*.

6 THE KNIGHT AS STORY-TELLER

In shaping their stories authors frequently adopt the perspective of one or another of their characters, so that we see events through the eyes of those characters and, while we are reading, adopt their values – even though they may not coincide completely with our own (Jane Austen is a good example of a writer who tells her stories from the perspective of her heroines). Sometimes authors use a first person narrative where we hear the story from the mouth of a character who may or may not be a reliable judge (Lockwood in *Wuthering Heights* is a narrator whom we obviously cannot trust). In this kind of case we may be at least as much preoccupied with the character telling the story as with the actual events he recounts.

The *Knight's Tale* is of course, *formally* told by the Knight so that we have to consider the question of his 'reliability'; to decide whether Chaucer is asking us to accept or to question the perspective of his character-narrator. You will have noticed that throughout the commentary I have referred to 'the narrator' rather than to 'the Knight' or to 'Chaucer'. This is because there is some disagreement among critics about the relation of the tale to its fictional teller.

Some hold that since the *Knight's Tale* was probably written before the *Canterbury Tales* were planned (we have a reference to an early work about Palamon and Arcite) its perspective is that of its author, and there are no practical implications in Chaucer's assigning it to the Knight. This argument seems unsatisfactory. First, we have no way of knowing how the early tale may have been altered before its inclusion in the larger work; more importantly, Chaucer chose to assign it to the Knight in a section of the *Canterbury Tales* which lays much emphasis on the characters of the pilgrims, and on the interactions between them.

Other critics take the Knight as a reliable narrator, whose judgement we must accept, because they claim he represents a religious ideal of chivalry, fighting for his faith on the frontiers of Christianity, and holding to the central values of his society 'Trouthe and honour, fredom and curteisie' (I 46).

Fairly recently, however, critics have begun to question the Knight's reliability. Their arguments take into account both the portrait in the *General Prologue* and features of the tale itself. One commentator, indeed, has argued that the portrait is heavily ironic, and that the Knight emerges as a low-class mercenary; the kind of soldier who presented a problem all over Europe at the time. Most of the arguments for this point of view seem rather unconvincing, not least because the pilgrims are shown to be outstanding examples of their social groups rather than social outcasts. However, the case rests heavily on a valuable analysis of the battles we are told the Knight has fought, and this suggests that Chaucer's contemporaries would have been less ready than some modern critics to accept him as a religious ideal.

The battle of Alexandria (1365) was known as a massacre of Christians as well as heathens, and the siege of Algezir, 1342–4 (modern Algeciras in the Moorish kingdom of Granada in Spain) was neither particularly successful, nor seen as part of a holy war. The Knight's fighting in Tramyssene (Tlemcen in Algeria) and Palatye (Balat in Turkey) would have been in the service of one heathen against another, and the same is probably true of his exploits in Belmarye (Morocco and part of modern Algeria), for there seems to have been no crusading activity there. Russia was Christian by this time, and the form of words Chaucer uses cannot easily be taken to mean that the Knight fought for the Russians.

Other features of the portrait seem to separate the Knight from a religious ideal; the emphasis on the formal honours he has received 'Ful ofte tyme he hadde the bord bigonne' (I 52), suggests a concern with worldly reputation, and the 'mortal batailles' (probably single combats in this context) and tournaments he has fought in were disapproved of by the Church.

However, there is nothing to distinguish the Knight's activities from those of some of the great lords of the country to whom fighting was a prestigious as well as a profitable activity. He seems, then, typical of his social group rather than an outsider from it. Moreover, it is hard to see the lavish praise heaped on him by the pilgrim-narrator as completely ironic.

We need, however, to consider what it is that this narrator chooses to admire. *Worthy* is a word which recurs noticeably in the description, and the first, rather general, use 'a worthy man' seems to suggest the Knight as morally good. However, later uses are more specific; the Knight is 'ful worthy' in 'his lordes werre' and is described as a 'worthy knyght' straight after his military exploits have been listed. In these contexts the word has much more the force of 'efficient', 'effective', 'good at one's job'. The final use seems to insist on this sense. 'And though that he were worthy, he was wys' (I 68). Here the odd disjunctive 'though' suggests that the Knight's kind of worthiness does not necessarily imply wisdom, that in fact being wise and being a good fighter is unusual. The Knight, then, is praised almost exclusively for his efficiency as a fighter, and as we have seen, the causes for which he fights do not seem to be particularly important.

The other qualities for which the Knight is praised are, like his fighting, not necessarily moral. *Wysdom* has a wide range of uses in Middle English; the Knight *may* be 'wise' in our sense of the word, he may, however, be no more than prudent or even calculating. His mild manners 'of his port as meeke as is a mayde' and his polite speech 'He nevere yet no vileynye ne sayde' may be taken as implying moral qualities, but we are not *told* that they do. All we really know is that he has proper courtly manners. The climactic line of praise 'He was a verray, parfit, gentil knyght' (I 72), is similarly open. We may take it to mean that he is an epitome of moral perfection, or just that he is a perfect example of noble behaviour.

The reason for this openness, I think, is the narrator's silence about the general usefulness of the Knight's activities and qualities. This silence seems to suggest that we are not to take him as an estates ideal, for in estates literature the function of the Knight is to protect the weak and helpless.

If we look at the description, not in isolation, but in relation to the rest of the *General Prologue* we may reflect, too, that the narrator's lavish praise of all of his fellow pilgrims emerges as, at the least, undiscriminating.

We need to take into account also those distancing devices I have noticed in the tale itself, for it is not just that the Knight distances us from some of his characters, but we are likely also to feel some unease at the contradictory picture of divine order he presents, and indeed at the seeming incapacity of Theseus (who is the Knight's hero) to create an order which does not depend on destruction.

My view, then, is that while the Knight's portrait in the *General Prologue* is emphatically not satirical, he, like the rest of the pilgrims, is shown as a limited, and therefore not completely reliable narrator; that Chaucer distances us from the Knight's perspective so that we can think about and question the values which the tale embodies and the Knight's social group adheres to. This questioning is, of course, pointed in the reactions of the pilgrims to his tale and to that of the churlish Miller who 'quites' it.

7 SPECIMEN PASSAGE AND CRITICAL COMMENTARY

7.1 SPECIMEN PASSAGE

The Temple of Mars

> First on the wal was peynted a forest,
> In which ther dwelleth neither man ne best,
> With knotty, knarry, bareyne trees olde,
> Of stubbes sharpe and hidouse to biholde,
> In which ther ran a rumbel in a swough,
> As though a storm sholde bresten every bough.
> And dounward from an hille, under a bente,
> Ther stood the temple of Mars armypotente,
> Wroght al of burned steel, of which the entree
> Was long and streit, and gastly for to see.   10
> And therout came a rage and swich a veze
> That it made al the gate for to rese.
> The northren lyght in at the dores shoon,
> For wyndowe on the wal ne was ther noon,
> Thurgh which men myghten any light discerne.
> The dore was al of adamant eterne,
> Yclenched overthwart and endelong
> With iren tough; and for to make it strong,
> Every pyler, the temple to sustene,
> Was tonne-greet, of iren bright and shene.   20
>   Ther saugh I first the derke ymaginyng
> Of Felonye, and al the compassyng;
> The crueel Ire, reed as any gleede;
> The pykepurs, and eek the pale Drede;
> The smylere with the knyf under the cloke;
> The shepne brennynge with the blake smoke;

The tresoun of the mordrynge in the bedde;
The open werre, with woundes al bibledde;
Contek, with blody knyf and sharp manace.
Al ful of chirkyng was that sory place.   30
The sleere of hymself yet saugh I ther, –
His herte-blood hath bathed al his heer;
The nayl ydryven in the shode a-nyght;
The colde deeth, with mouth gapyng upright.
Amyddes of the temple sat Meschaunce,
With disconfort and sory contenaunce.
Yet saugh I Woodnesse, laughynge in his rage,
Armed Compleint, Outhees, and fiers Outrage;
The careyne in the busk, with throte ycorve;
A thousand slayn, and nat of qualm ystorve;   40
The tiraunt, with the pray by force yraft;
The toun destroyed, ther was no thyng laft.
Yet saugh I brent the shippes hoppesteres;
The hunte strangled with the wilde beres;
The sowe freten the child right in the cradel;
The cook yscalded, for al his longe ladel.

7.2 CRITICAL COMMENTARY

This passage is only a part of the description of the temple of Mars,
erected by Theseus in the list where Palamon and Arcite are to fight.
The passage enforces the destructiveness of Mars, both as god of war
and as 'infortunate' planet. Its subject is claimed to be the painting on
the walls of the temple 'First on the wal was *peynted* a forest' (1). The
perspective on the scene is that of an eye witness so that we are
constantly aware of the effect of the temple on a viewer trying to take
in every detail: Ther saugh I . . . (21) . . . yet saugh I ther (31) Yet
saugh I . . . (37) Yet saugh I . . . (43). While this device is clearly a
dramatic impropriety, for our medieval knight is telling a story set in
classical Greece, it has the effect of placing us with the narrator as we
attempt to take in the scene. It adds, too, a slightly disorientating
touch, gives us a sense that there is something odd at work.

Our disorientation, slight at first, grows as the passage continues
and the distinction between the real temple in the lists and the temple
painted on its walls becomes more and more blurred. The process by
which the paintings cease to be shown as visual, static objects begins
when we are told that in the painted forest 'ther dwelleth neither man
ne best' (2). The word *dwelleth*, implying a continuation in time,

takes us immediately outside the range of what can literally be said of a painting, and the vivid description of the forest in which one adjective is piled upon another – *knotty*, *knarry*, *bareyne* – appeals to our sense of touch as much as to our eyesight. The alliteration of *knotty*, *knarry* seems to insist on the hardness of the trees, a hardness which is enforced by the use of *sharpe* in the next line. We are further disorientated when the painted forest moves and is filled with noise:

> ther ran a rumbel in a swough,
> As though a storm sholde bresten every bough
>
> (5–6)

Each stage of the description seems to take us further and further away from the static painting the passage purports to describe.

After the forest surrounding it we are shown the temple of Mars in Thrace, and again the painting is given a three-dimensional quality, partly by the way in which the precise positioning of the temple creates a sense of perspective – 'dounward from an hille, under a bente' (7) – partly by the solidity with which the temple, 'wroght al of burned steel', is invested. This three-dimensional effect is quickly followed by descriptions of violent movement so that the blast, the *rage* and *veze*, which issues from the temple door destroys both the stasis and solidity of the picture as the gates which are its subject begin to tremble. It is as though we have left behind the temple in the lists and been taken straight into the reality of what is depicted on its walls.

In the next lines our disorientation is complete, for the doors through which the northern light filters seem to be those of the pictured temple, and yet suddenly we are taken inside, drawn in through these representations of doors to penetrate, in a rather looking-glass effect, what does not really lie behind them:

> For wyndowe on the wal ne was ther noon,
> Thurgh which men myghten any light discerne.
>
> (14–15)

We cannot easily assume, either, that we have been taken back to the 'real' temple in the lists, for the light coming through the doors is a *northern* light which seems to belong to the 'colde, frosty regioun' of the painted temple and not to that built on the *west* side of the lists. Our confusion is maintained, for there is nothing except the shift from the plural *dores* of 13 to the singular *dore* of 16 to suggest the latter is that of the 'real' temple, and yet the stress is all on its solidity, strength and weight. The repetition of heavy, three-syllable words – *overthwart, endelong*; the enjambment 'endelong/ With iren tough' which directs our attention to the strength of the material reinforcing the door; the way in which the verb *Yclenched* is stressed by its appearance at the beginning of a line, convey, not the *appearance* of strength, but a sense of something that is actually strong. The *tonne-greet* pillars of the temple (but which temple?) maintain this emphasis and we are not returned to the visual until the reference to 'iren bright and shene'.

In the next lines the perception that we are back in the temple of the lists gradually asserts itself as further paintings on its walls are described, this time, on the whole, in such terms as establish them as pictures, though the first; 'the derke ymaginyng/ Of Felonye, and al the compassyng' seems impossible to represent visually. How does one paint an *ymaginyng*, a dark thought?

The disorientation which the passage has induced in us up to this point, the way in which we are, quite literally, unable to tell where we are, is a powerful means of creating a sense of Mars as an immediate force. It is as though we are taken to the very seat of his activity and are shown, not men's ways of representing them, but his operations in themselves.

The personifications which follow the description of Felonye are a mixture of abstractions – Ire, Contek, Woodnesse, and representative figures or events – 'the sleere of hymself', 'the toun destroyed'. Frequently the abstractions are made vivid by a brief, emblematic description – 'Contek' with blody knyf and sharp manace', 'Woodnesse, laughynge in his rage'; sometimes one effective, defining adjective is used of them – 'pale Drede', 'fiers Outrage'; once they become part of a list 'Armed Compleint, Outhees, and fiers Outrage' as though there are so many of Mars's attributes that there is no time to describe them all. A sense of the overwhelming power of Mars and of the pervasiveness of his influence is conveyed also by the way in which abstract personifications and representative figures and scenes are mingled with one another so that we move backward and forward between single menacing figures and small scenes in which that menace is manifested.

The passage emphasises the physical details of death and destruction 'His herte-blood hath bathed al his heer' (32) 'The colde deeth, with mouth gapyng upright' (34). Moreover, the activities of Mars are not limited to purposeful violence, but include the violent and horrible accident; 'The sowe freten the child right in the cradel'. The unpleasantness of this image lies not only in the revulsion we feel at the child being destroyed by a beast, but in the insecurity it breeds, for the child is attacked by the familiar and domestic in the very place it should be safe. This movement into domestic accident insists on Mars as a planetary force and extends his sphere of influence so that no one is safe from him; the range of his activities is brought out by the parallelism of the line openings

> The hunte strangled . . .
> The sowe freten . . .
> The cook yscalded . . .   (44–45)

All the details of the passage combine to create a scene of peculiar vividness. Even those effects which seem designed to disorientate the reader do not confuse the picture, but lend it a nightmarish quality. One might feel, and here we are helped by the eye-witness perspective, that far from being the description of a physical temple, the passage is a visionary account of the workings of the narrator's real god.

Like the rest of the *Knight's Tale*, this passage is written in rhyming couplets, with a basic pattern of five stresses to the line. Chaucer handles the form with his characteristic flexibility; whatever the grand effect created the verse never loses touch with the rhythms of speech. Line pattern and sentence structure are held in tension so that there is no lapse into metrical monotony: for example, the enjambment between lines 9 and 10, 17 and 18, 21 and 22 carries the flow of the sentence across the line endings, while the movement of lines 18, 40, 41 and 42 is broken with strong caesuras, each marking the beginning of a new grammatical unit.

Chaucer's delicate and varied use of rhyme also helps to ensure that the metrical pattern never becomes too obstructive; single-syllabled words are frequently rhymed with double-syllabled – *olde/biholde, bedde/bibledde, manace/place*, there is some use of feminine (unstressed) rhymes – *Hoppesteres/beres*, and of double rhymes – *cradel/ladel*.

Above all, it is important to emphasise that Chaucer's metrical patterns are functional, designed to enforce his sense rather than to impress us with their brilliance. Thus, the flat, metrical regularity of the one-line sentence 'Al ful of chirkyng was that sory place' by breaking the parallelism of lines 25–29 punctuates and summarises the catalogue of Mars's destructive manifestations, making the resumption of that catalogue all the more powerful.

To speak with any particularity of Chaucer's versification – and particularity is necessary if we are to say anything at all – will inevitably take us into a discussion of his sense.

8 CRITICAL RECEPTION

Chaucer's poetry has been consistently admired from his own time down to ours. His contemporaries praised him for his rhetorical skill, his learning, his love poetry and his translations. Significantly Deschamps, writing around 1386, in comparing him to such figures of the past as Socrates and Ovid conferred on him the status of an *auctor* (see 1.6).

Although succeeding generations have sometimes chosen to stress other characteristics of his work there is an unusual consensus about his quality. On the whole Chaucer's impact on the English language, his skill in characterisation and his status as a 'moral' poet have always been recognised.

To his immediate successors Chaucer was a master, and his style was widely imitated. John Lydgate, writing around twenty years after Chaucer's death, calls him

> Floure of poetes thorghout Breteyne,
> Which sothly hadde most of excellence
> In rethorike and in eloquence

This judgement is echoed in 1503 by the Scottish poet William Dunbar:

> O reverend Chaucere, rose of rethoris all,
> As in oure tong ane flour imperiall.

With the Renaissance, opinions became more divided for the past many writers referred back to was the past of classical antiquity which they considered themselves to have discovered. Thus, although Edmund Spenser calls Chaucer 'well of English undefyled', Sir Philip

Sidney writing in the same period, the late sixteenth century, is more measured in his praise:

> I know not whether to marvel more, either that he in that misty time could see so clearly, or that we in this clear age walk so stumblingly after him. Yet had he great wants, fit to be forgiven in so reverend antiquity.

Dryden, writing at the beginning of the eighteenth century, claims for Chaucer a special place in our history – 'from Chaucer the purity of the English tongue began' – and saw him as obeying one of the great imperatives of Dryden's own age – 'Chaucer followed nature everywhere . . . ' Of the *Canterbury Tales* he remarked

> he has taken . . . the various manners . . . of the whole English nation, in his age . . . We have our forefathers and great-grand-dames all before us, as they were in Chaucer's days; their general characters are still remaining in mankind, and even in England

Dryden's view of Chaucer was shared by many later critics, including William Blake (see Introduction), and John Ruskin who voiced a nineteenth-century patriotism in claiming Chaucer's as 'the most perfect type of a true English mind'. Writing just a little later, Matthew Arnold praised him for 'his large, free, simple, clear yet kindly view of human life', but judged that in comparison with the greatest poets Chaucer lacked 'high seriousness'. All these views have had their influence on twentieth-century critics; at the beginning of the century Chaucer's realism was heavily stressed, notably by J. M. Manly, who attempted to find real-life originals for many of the pilgrims of the *Canterbury Tales*. Recent criticism, however, has tended to emphasise his literariness, and J. Mann in her influential book, *Chaucer and Medieval Estates Satire*, has shown how the apparently individual figures of the pilgrims exploit the social stereotypes of the age, while much interesting work has been produced on Chaucer's use of such writers as Boccaccio.

During the century the *Canterbury Tales* has received much attention from scholars and critics who have expressed widely differing views on the work. At the risk of over-simplification it seems possible to identify certain trends and patterns within this diversity of opinion.

Perhaps the most established reading of the *Canterbury Tales* takes the work as a unity, with its individual tales related not only to their tellers, but also to one another. Many of those who hold this view suggest that Chaucer uses as an organising principle such oppositions as experience and authority, freedom and necessity, art and morality. There is also something of a consensus that Chaucer finally abandons the ironies created by these oppositions and adopts an affirmative, religious, ultimately authoritarian stance in keeping with the certainties they discern in the thought of the period. Such readings usually take the Knight and Parson as embodying the secular and religious ideals of the age and thus providing a standard against which the views of the other pilgrims must be judged.

Recently, however, both the conception of the *Canterbury Tales* as a unity and the notion that Chaucer expresses 'medieval certainties' have been attacked. Some scholars have argued, using the Hengwrt manuscript to support their case, that the *Canterbury Tales* are a loosely linked collection of stories with no strong organising themes. A number of critics, some influenced by an awareness of the tensions and upheavals of the fourteenth century, have come to regard Chaucer as a poet profoundly sceptical of the social and religious structures of his day. Such critics see Chaucer as affirming no authoritative truths, but as exposing the conflicts and uncertainties of his society.

It is perhaps a measure of Chaucer's richness that each generation of critics creates him afresh.

REVISION QUESTIONS

1. How far do you think the *Knight's Tale* suits its teller as he is described in the *General Prologue*?

2. In what ways are the gods important to the *Knight's Tale*?

3. How does the way in which the tale is told affect our judgement of the central characters and events in the *Knight's Tale*?

4. Consider the different means by which characters are presented in the *Knight's Tale*.

5. 'The *Knight's Tale* offers us a world which humans are powerless to make sense of.' How far do you agree with this comment?

6. 'Out of all the characters in the *Knight's Tale*, Theseus alone is active. The rest are passive victims.' Do you agree?

7. How similar are the characters of Arcite and Palamon?

FURTHER READING

Text

If you wish to read more of the *Canterbury Tales* the standard text is
F. N. Robinson (ed.), *The Works of Geoffrey Chaucer*, 2nd edn
(Oxford University Press, 1957).

Critical studies and background reading

While there is no substitute for a thorough knowledge of the text
itself, a small amount of further reading is often helpful for the
knowledge it supplies and, most importantly, for the questions it
raises about the work. Some of the books listed below contain more
information about Chaucer and his world, others, chapters speci-
fically on the *Knight's Tale*.

J. A. Burrow (ed.), *Geoffrey Chaucer: A Critical Anthology* (Pen-
   guin, 1969) This contains a useful and influential study by R.
   Neuse of the *Knight's Tale*.
B. Ford (ed.), *The New Pelican Guide to English Literature, vol. 1:
   Medieval Literature* (2 books) (Penguin, 1983).
N. Havely, *Chaucer's Boccaccio*, D. S. Brewer (Rowman & Little-
   field, 1980) This contains a translation of parts of the *Teseida* if
   you are interested in looking more closely at how Chaucer used
   that work.
G. Kane, *Chaucer*, Past Masters series (Oxford University Press,
   1984).
C. Muscatine, *Chaucer and the French Tradition* (University of
   California Press, 1957).
I. Robinson, *Chaucer and the English Tradition* (Cambridge University Press, 1972).
J. J. Anderson (ed.), *The Canterbury Tales*, Casebook Series (Macmillan, 1974).